Memoirs of A Sailor

1940-1946

Alvin E. DuBois

TABLE OF CONTENTS

JOIN THE NAVY-LEARN A TRADE 4
Roger Bergin, Pat Othout 4
We left Detroit for Great Lakes, Illinois........... 6
Pay and your expenses during Training 9
Transferred to Bremerton, Washington 20
First set eyes on the USS Pennsylvania........... 21
Standing watch...................................... 26
Facts about the USS Pennsylvania BB38 Fleet Flagship.. 29
Learn how to refuel at sea 33
Catapulting and retrieving a plane at sea 34
Admiral Husband E Kimmel relieved Admiral James O. Richardson............................... 39
Black Cat Café 41
I decided to go out for boxing 49
Menu for July 4, 1941 53
Thanksgiving Menu 1941 55
December 7, 1941 61
Royal Oak sailor gave life 71
Report of the action of December 7th 72
High Altitude Bombing Attack......................... 76
Flooding of drydock... 77
Fire in the dock 77
Damage to Pennsylvania 78

Distinguished Conduct	81
Repairs	81
Deep-sea diving school	91
40mm shell casing makes a pretty lamp	97
Admiral Pye	98
On our way to the Aleutian Islands	99
Transfer to Treasure Island	120
USS Ross (DD563)	127
Attack on Saipan and Tinian	137
Shellbacks serve subpoenas	143
On our way to Leyte Gulf	155
Leyte Gulf	158
The night of the Great Battle	182
On our way home	199
Summary	204
Typhoon in Yokohama Bay	210
My Future Wife	212
Getting the ship ready for the Mothball Fleet	215
Honorable Discharge	220
Conclusion	224
Fate	225

"JOIN THE NAVY –LEARN A TRADE

I graduated from high school in June of 1940. That summer I rode motorcycle with a sidecar for a wholesale tool company delivering tools to different factories throughout the city of Detroit. I realized that I couldn't do this for the rest of my life. There were three of us. Roger Bergin, Pat Othout, and myself riding motorcycle together after working hours. None of us had a very good job, so we talked about joining one of the armed services. I wanted the Army and the others preferred the Navy. At that time the US Navy was advertising on billboards and newspapers using the motto, "Join the Navy and learn a trade", the Navy won.

We went to the recruiting office in Detroit and talked to the naval recruiter. His information regarding a naval career sounded good to us, so we agreed to return the following week to fill out an application and take a physical examination, which we did. One of the questions was "Have you ever committed a misdemeanor or a felony? " I answered "No."

We went to another office to take our physical. There were about twenty-five of us in there, and the first thing they demanded was for us to take off our clothes, I wasn't used to doing that with others around. I watched the other fellows and they started to undress, so I followed suit. The next order was for us to bend over and grab our ankles that just about did it! I wasn't sure that I wanted to join the Navy. That day finally came to an end. We went home and waited for them to call us. After a week Roger was called. Pat and I didn't get a call for another week.

    A recruiter came to my house to see me and to talk with my parents, during the talk he questioned my answer to the misdemeanor and the felony questions on my application. He told me that I almost didn't get in because I had lied about that. I replied that I hadn't robbed a bank or held anyone up, nor had I done any breaking and entering. He agreed that I was correct about that, but he asked about the nineteen speeding tickets that I had received in the past seventeen months. My Dad hollered, "What!" It was obvious that my Dad didn't know anything about these speeding tickets, as I had always paid the fines without my Dad being aware of them. Finally I was accepted into the Navy a week later than Roger.

Roger was born in Saskatchewan, Canada. When he was fourteen he moved to a small town near Flint, Michigan where he lived with, and was raised by an uncle. When he was about nineteen, he moved to Royal Oak, Michigan, and that was where I met him. That was all I knew about his background. He was twenty-two and I was eighteen when we joined the Navy.

The morning that we left Detroit for Great Lakes, Illinois, was the first time I had ever been on a train, and I thought this was neat. There were about fifty recruits on the train going to Great Lakes. Most of us were eighteen to twenty years of age, and most of us had never been on our own. When we had to change train stations in Chicago, we really didn't know how to go about it. We lost some of our cockiness right then. We arrived at Great Lakes about 9:00pm. They issued us our sea bags, (our uniforms and clothing) and our hammock. This hammock is what substituted for a bed for the next eighteen months. That night we were supposed to sleep in our hammocks. We had to string them between two pipes that were about forty inches from the floor. This wasn't hard to do, but trying to get into them was. There was nothing overhead to hang onto and nothing beside us. I would say about half of us managed to get into them, and the other half slept on the floor. Before morning there were a lot more who had fallen out of them during the night. Every time someone turned over they fell out.

    The next morning we fell out for muster (roll call), and marched to the mess hall for breakfast. I wasn't used to eating what they served. After breakfast we went back to our barracks. The chief, that was to be our company commander for the next five weeks, gave us an outline of things to expect. At that point I was sure that I had made a mistake by joining the Navy. When we fell out from quarters, we went to get a haircut, it didn't matter whether or not you had one yesterday; you still had to get one today. It took about three minutes a head. The hair was about 1/2 inch long when they finished. Most of the time while in boot camp, we were either marching, doing close order drill, or standing inspection. On the third day they gave us a memo about our pay and expenses during our training period.

UNITED STATES NAVAL TRAINING STATION

GREAT LAKES ILLINOIS

NM3/L16
63/rt

November 19, 1940

COMMANDING OFFICER'S MEMORANDUM NUMBER 15-40 TO ALL RECRUITS

Subject: Your pay and your expenses during Training based on five-week training period.

   1.   Your rate of pay while in training is seventy cents (70¢) per day. While you are on leave your pay is increased to one dollar and twelve cents ($1.12) per day, because while on leave you receive 42¢ ration money in addition to your pay of 70¢

   2.   As soon as you enter the Training

Station, and before you have earned any pay, you are issued two ship's service coupon books amounting to seven dollars ($7.00) altogether. You will be required to pay for these books later on, and the money to do so will come out of your earnings. The first of these books contains two dollars ($2.00) in coupons, and is to be used for essential services during your training period as listed below:

1st hair cut	$0.15
Hair cut, 3rd week	.25
Hair cut, 5th week	.25
Hair cut, after leave	.25
Laundry, bag & hammock, 4th week	.25
Laundry, bag & hammock, after leave	.25
Tailor, blues cleaned	.50
Total	$1.90

The second of these books contains five dollars ($5.00) in coupons and is to be used to purchase certain necessary items not furnished by the Government and which you must pay for yourself, as listed:

Blue jackets' Manual	$1.62
One can shoe polish	.08

Two bars laundry soap	.08
Two bars toilet soap	.16
Soap box	.21
Tooth paste	.10
Alterations to clothing	.40
Stamps and stationery	.55
Total	$3.20

This leaves you $1.80 in the book which can be used for cigarettes, candy, photographs, etc., and you will be wise to save some of your coupons for such expenses.

   3. At the end of your detention period of twenty-one days, you will have earned $14.70. At that time you will be paid five dollars ($5.00) in cash. About $3.25 of this should be used to pay your first insurance premium; you will have remaining about $1.75 in cash for miscellaneous expenses.

      This leaves you about nine dollars ($9.00) on the books; and you still owe seven ($7.00) for the two coupon books advanced you on the first day.

4. During your second phase of training, following detention, you earn $12.60, which, added to what previously remained on the books for you, totals about $22.00. From this the paymaster must deduct the money for your second insurance premium, and for the hospital fund, leaving you about $17.00. The day you graduate this entire amount will be paid you in cash and with it you must purchase your round trip ticket to go home on leave. You still owe seven dollars ($7.00) for the two coupon books.

5. While you are on leave you earn $9.66. When you return from leave and prepare to go to sea, you will be paid ten dollars ($10.00). Seven dollars ($7.00) of this will be required to pay for the coupon books for which you still owe; the remainder you may have to use as you wish during transit to your new duty.

6. Please note that those figures are average and there may be variations from them one way or another in individual cases.

7. It should be evident that every cent of your earning is required for the expenses you normally incur during training. You must be extremely <u>frugal or you will not have sufficient money to go home on leave and to pay your debt.</u> There is no objection to your receiving money from home if your parents wish to send it to you. However, you must not expect it and must be prepared to carry your expenses on your own earnings.

8. The substance of the above paragraphs is stated below in different form. Perhaps this summary will be easier to read and analyze:

(a) ASSUMPTIONS:

1. That the recruit arrives without cash funds.
2. That the recruit will desire to return home on nine days leave including travel time.
3. That each recruit will have to meet certain necessary expenses while at the Station under training and while in route to the Fleet in addition to the expenses of his visit home on recruit graduation leave.
4. That some money will be required for liberty purposes – for liberties after completion of detention and up to date of departure on leave, and miscellaneous items of canteen merchandise.
5. That the great majority of recruits will purchase National Service Life Insurance in suitable amounts.

2. Therefore to enlighten recruits who may or may not visualize the above assumptions,

considering their inexperience at budgeting funds, and to train them to be frugal, the following budget, applicable to a five-week training period and incorporating a workable relationship between income and output, is offered for guidance.

PAY	INCOME	EXPENDITURE	BALANCE AVAILABLE
		$7.00	(-)$7.00 (Note1)
0-21 (In detention)	$14.70 (Note 2)	5.00 (Note 3)	2.70
21-39 (2nd Phase of training)	12.60 (Note 4)	3.50 (Note 5)	11.80
39		17.00 (Note 6)	(-)5.20
39-48 (Recruit Leave Period)	9.66 (Note 7)		
48-50 (Preparation to go to sea)	1.40 (Note 8)	3.00 (Note 9)	2.86 (Note 10)

NOTE 1 –This amount is advanced to recruit by ship's service in the form of coupon books to cover his expenses

15

for essential services and for auxiliary equipment necessary but not furnished by the Government. He must refund this amount to ship's service after he returns from leave.

NOTE 2 - This amount represents 21 days earning at 70¢ per day.

NOTE 3 – This $5.00 is paid in cash to recruit at end of detention period. With it he will be able to pay about $3.25 National Service Life Insurance premium; assuming he has subscribed to a $5,000.00 policy, the remaining $1.75 he may use for pocket money.

NOTE 4 – This amount represents his earnings during second phase of training.

NOTE 5 – This amount is deducted from recruits' pay by the paymaster to pay his second National Service Life Insurance premium and his hospital fund.

NOTE 6 – This is the approximate amount remaining to the average recruit's credit, and will be paid to the recruit on graduation. With it he must purchase his ticket to go and return on leave and provide his pocket money.

NOTE 7 – This amount represents recruit's earnings during nine days leave:

> 9 days pay @ 70¢ $6.30
> 8 days rations @ 42¢   3.36
> $9.66

NOTE 8 – This amount represents recruit's earnings during two days during which he will prepare to go to sea.

NOTE 9 – The recruit is paid ten dollars ($10.00) on return from leave. Seven dollars ($7.00) he must refund to ship's service (see Note 1 above) leaving a balance of three dollars ($3.00) for pocket money while traveling to his new station.

NOTE 10 This approximate amount remains on recruit's pay account and is transferred to his new paymaster.

JOHN DOWNES,
Rear Admiral, U. S. Navy.

NOTE: The above budget applies to members of Companies 92 to 126 inclusive, based on the assumption that six new companies will be formed each week during the month of November 1940.

When a person enlisted in the Navy, he went in as an apprentice seaman. The pay was $21.00 a month. After four months he was promoted to seaman 2nd class. His pay increased to $36.00 a month. After that promotion it depends a lot upon the Individual. It was up to them to study for their next rate. He had to spend a specified amount of time in his old rate, and then he had to pass a written examination for the new rate. The following is a pay scale at 1940 rates per month. Seaman 1st class $54.00, Petty officer 3rd class $62.00, P.O. 2nd class $74.00, PO 1st class $86.00. Chief acting appointment $99.00 and Chief Permanent appointment $126.00. There was an additional 5 percent for each four years of service. In February, my pay went to $36.00, which was a $15.00 a month increase. One could live high on the hog as long as he didn't do much.

I believe the main thing they wanted to teach us was discipline and how to follow orders. The two main things I learned was to refrain from volunteering for anything, and when someone with authority gave me an order, I didn't ask why. Except for a couple of minor incidents, I got through boot camp in good shape. I only saw Roger twice while we were there.

At the end of the five week period, we were given a ten day leave so we could go home, I had a wonderful time during those ten days. My brother loaned me his motorcycle, and I saw a lot of friends.

When I returned to Great Lakes, I was transferred to Bremerton, Washington. Roger had already been transferred to the USS Arizona. I was assigned to the sister ship the USS Pennsylvania they were both battleships. The trip to Bremerton took two nights and three days. All of the sailors went by train, occupying two coaches. The rest of the passengers were civilians. It was beautiful! This was the first time that I had seen the Rocky Mountains, I guess I fell in love with them. I thought they were the most beautiful, majestic works of nature that I had ever seen. We arrived in Seattle early in the morning and had to wait for a ferry to take us to Bremerton.

When I first set eyes on the USS Pennsylvania (Pennsy), I couldn't see how anything so large, made of iron could possibly float.

It was the largest ship I had ever seen, There were a lot of large ships tied up at the dock, and they were all in for repairs, some minor, and some requiring a major overhaul.

The Pennsylvania had been there for three months, and had one more month to go. When I first went aboard ship, I was assigned to the second division. The living quarters and the work area was forward of the main mast. It was known as a deck division.

I will never forget the first day I went down to the head (restroom). They were on the main deck all the way to the bow. It was hot and the toilets were nothing but a long trough with some boards fixed to the trough on hinges. You either sat on the boards or you could raise them. On one end of the trough seawater was being pumped into it, and the other end was the discharge end, where the waste was going through. If the discharge line got plugged, the water would run over the top. The first day it was plugged. There was no privacy whatsoever. Aboard ship they don't know what the word means.

That night after work we went in to take showers about 5 o'clock pm. The showers were in the compartment side of the head. There were probably twenty-five to thirty fellows taking showers. You would get under the water, get wetted down, then step back and let the next guy in while you soaped down, then get back into the shower to rinse. Fresh water is a precious commodity aboard ship, if you wasted fresh water, someone would tell you about it.

After we had taken our showers, we went to

our compartment to eat family style. The petty officer in charge of the table would help himself first, and then the others could do the same. You were to take a medium-sized helping the first time until everyone was served. If you wanted more, and there was none, the mess cook would go to the galley for more. I always had enough to eat.

After we finished eating, we got our sea bags and started to put our gear in the locker that had been assigned to us. Any time after 9:00pm we could put up our hammock and go to bed. By this time we were quite accomplished at putting up our hammocks and sleeping in them. I lay in mine wondering what I had gotten myself into. I didn't lie there very long until I fell asleep; I was so tired.

The next morning reveille sounded at 6:00am. We cleaned up, ate breakfast, and fell out for muster. We were told that most of us would be transferred to another division the next day. We would not have any duty that day, but we should familiarize ourselves with the ship, and to stay out of other people's way.

A couple of us went together, and we got

lost. We got kicked out of the engine room and the electrical repair shop. We started to go down into a gun turret, and was stopped before we even got started. The one thing to do when you are lost aboard ship is to go up, and sooner or later you will come to the topside. The Pennsy had three decks, and she also had three compartments below decks. The difference between a deck and a compartment is that you must go up and down to get from one compartment to the other. This is to help prevent flooding. All compartments are supposed to be water tight, in order not to flood from one to the other. That was an interesting and a good day.

The next morning after muster, I was transferred to the 6B division. The living quarters were in a casemate, along with a 5"/51 caliber broad side gun. I ate and slept there for the next year. The 6B division was an anti-aircraft unit. Being apprentice seaman, we were given all the jobs that no one else wanted, such as washing the paint, chipping paint where there were rust spots, painting and scrubbing the decks with holly stones.

The decks were made of wood, and by holly stoning, you could get them almost white. The decks were scrubbed every day in port and the bad spots were holly stoned.

Another job no one volunteered for was a side cleaner's job. This consists of chipping paint and repainting the bare spots, but this time you are over the side of the ship in a boatswain's chair. A boatswain's chair is a short, flat board attached at the ends to a bridle of ropes to be used as a seat for a seaman working where there is no foothold. At one time or another I got in on all those good jobs, but I certainly didn't volunteer for them.

By this time it was getting close to Christmas, and I was a little homesick. It never was really cold here but it rained a lot this time of year. However, on either December 21st or 23rd we did have a few snow flurries. They didn't last, but we actually had some snow. This was my first Christmas away from home.

   We left the Navy yard at Bremerton for San Francisco on the 27th of December 1940. We were at sea for only two days and we only spent four hours at San Francisco, which was just long enough to take on some ammunition. We left San Francisco on the 29th for San Pedro, which was two more days at sea. At this point I had forgotten what we had been through at boot camp, and all the dirty jobs that had been given us in the Navy yards. I liked going to sea. We spent seven days in San Pedro with two liberties, enjoying every minute of it. We left San Pedro on January 7,1941 for Hawaii, staying at sea for seven days, and enduring bad weather for five of them. Going to Hawaii was my first time "standing watch". I was to strike the bells every half-hour, not one minute before or not one minute after. Before I could strike the bells, I had to ask the officer of the deck permission to strike the bells, and he would say," Permission granted ". Striking the bells was a method of letting everyone know what time it was. The watch section was changed every four hours and the guys on watch were always waiting to be relieved.

    The day before we were to arrived in Hawaii, the weather became calm, and was beautiful. There was hardly a ripple on the water, which was so blue, and the sun was so bright, almost without a cloud in the sky. The next morning we could see land. Although the ocean had some swells, it wasn't rough and was really nice.

    As we came nearer to the island one could see the mountains and the green foliage, as we continued on we could see the beaches, which looked like white sand, but as we came closer we could see a lot of coral reefs. We came to the mouth of the channel, and as we started in a little further we began to see ships. The further we went the more ships we saw. As our ship went around Ford Island, we passed alot of ships that were anchored or tied up to buoys.

There were at least six other battleships, some light cruisers, destroyers, destroyer escorts, aircraft carriers, submarines, oil tankers, supply ships, repair ships, and even a hospital ship. As we continued around Ford Island, which is a Navy Air station, a couple of tugs met us and they pushed us over to the dock where we were to tie up. Later I learned that it was called 10-10 dock.

The Pennsy was the flagship of the pacific fleet; this had both its good and bad points. The good points were that she usually tied to a dock while in port instead of dropping anchor or tying to a buoy. This means that we could walk from the ship instead of taking a motor launch to shore. Another privilege was that we received the new movies when they were released. However, the appearance of the ship had to be in top shape at all times, and we had more regulations than the other ships, so our situation was more or less evened out.
I believe we were in port about four days before I had liberty, so on my first liberty I went to the Arizona to see my friend Roger. This was the first time we had been able to see

each other since we left boot camp. We made arrangements to meet the following Sunday at the front gate in order to go to Waikiki, which we did, and we had a great time.

The following are a few of the facts about the USS PENNSYLVANIA BB38 FLEET FLAGSHIP. She was the fleet flag until 1942. She was 600 feet long, with a 106-foot beam, and a displacement of 32,100 tons. There were

4-14 inch turrets of 3 guns each. They could shoot a projectile weighing 1,400 pounds at a distance of 20 miles. When one stood behind the turret, one could see the projectile flying through the air. They were never fired dead ahead or dead astern, as the recoil would be very hard on the hull of the ship. If all 12 guns fired broadside, it would probably move the ship about 6 feet backwards. They do not rapid-fire a large gun very often as the heat of the powder exploding, and it's weight going down the barrel would wear out the riflings. The guns are staggered-fired so they don't get too hot. Some of the other equipment aboard ship are: 10-5", 51 caliber broadside, 8-5, 25 caliber anti-aircraft guns, 4-3", 50 caliber anti-aircraft guns, and 4-50 caliber machine guns.

The ship carried approximately 1,800 men, 2 aircraft catapult, and three seaplanes of the KingFisher type.

The US Government maintains a Navy as the first line of defense. They had to have good ships along with trained men to run the ships. This is what we were doing in Hawaii; being trained to run our ship. When a person is being trained to do a new job, and is doing it for the first time, they are slow and awkward. This is the way we were. The more we did the job, the more proficient we were. We would go to sea for 4 or 5 days, and we would come back to port for 4 or 5 days Each time we went to sea, we were either doing something new or repeating a job we had already done.

When general quarters sounds, every man drops whatever he is doing, and goes to his designated station. Every man aboard ship has to go to his station as quickly as possible. All watertight doors have to be closed and dogged down, all the ammunition lockers are opened and ready to pass ammunition, and the smoking lamp is turned out, meaning no one can smoke. The gun covers are taken off, and the guns are ready to fire. Whatever our job is, we start to practice. It doesn't matter if we are a pointer, a trainer, a loader, an ammunition handler, we practice, practice, and practice. Then we secure from general quarters. Following general quarters we go back to the cleaning station where we had been before quarters sounded. We might only be back for a short time when air defense sounds. This means only the ones on anti-air defense stations have to go to quarters. More practice is involved.

There were other things we had to practice beside gunnery. We had to learn how to refuel at sea from a tanker while underway.

Sometimes we had to take another ship under tow because it was disabled, or we would catapult our seaplanes that were aboard and then retrieve them from the ocean. The Pennsy had to refuel the destroyers at sea. There would be a destroyer on the port side, and one on the starboard side, so the deck force could harness the three together by a method that held them well away from the battleship, while oil lines were passed to them in order for the oil to be pumped to them. This operation would take from an hour and a half to three hours, depending upon how rough the sea was, to how close one ship could get to the other. Needless to say, if the two ships ever rammed each other, there would be worse problems. Generally a gunners mate uses a shoulder gun (a line throwing gun) to get a light carrier line to the other ship. He might have to try more than once as the wind at times will carry the line off target. When the carrier line gets on the other ship it is hauled in. Larger messenger lines are sent over until they get the one that is large enough to tow the ship. The larger ship, such as a battleship, can take up to four hours to take each other in tow.

Catapulting and retrieving a plane at sea is one of the most fantastic things to watch. To catapult a plane from a battleship, the catapult is turned so the plane is headed into the wind. When the signal is given, a seaman picks up a six-inch cartridge case containing a powder charge. He holds it up to warn the pilot, and then inserts it into the catapult breech. The pilot gives the motor full power, and signals that he is ready to go. A gunners mate jerks the pin releasing the plane from the track. The catapult officer jerks the lanyard a second later catching the ship on an up roll. There is a blast from the motor, a detonation from the powder charge, and the plane shoots off the catapult at a mile a minute. The plane accelerates from a stand still to 60 miles per hour within the 60-foot length of the catapult, and the plane is in the air.

Retrieving a plane from the ocean is amazing. First the ship makes a wide semi-circle, ending up headed into the wind. This is done so the plane can land in the semi-circle where the sea is calm and the waves are not so high. The water is still rough, but not as rough as it is on the other side of the ship. A long rope is attached near the bow of the ship that trails back to about the quarter-deck. On the end of that rope is a sea sled, which has a webbing of ropes trailing behind. There is another line attached to the sea sled to keep it from drifting too far from the ship. When the plane lands, it should taxi up onto the sea sled and idle the motor. There is a hook on the bottom of the main pontoon, and that is to catch the webbing behind the sea sled, and consequently the plane is towed at the same speed as the ship. Then the crane from the ship swings out, and they lower the cable with a hook on the end fastening it to the plane and lifting it aboard. Sometimes when the plane lands in the water, the wing pontoon hits a wave too hard and bends it up. When that happens, the radioman has to get on the opposite wing and go out on the wing tip as far as he can, his weight helping to hold the wing with the good pontoon down, and it rides on the water. If he is not fast enough, the wing with the broken pontoon will dip into the ocean and turn over.

As the plane is rolling over, the pilot and the radioman get on the main pontoon and work themselves around the pontoon. The plane will end upside down and the two men will be on top of the main pontoon. The pontoon will keep the plane afloat regardless if it is right-side or bottom-side up. They still hook the cable to the plane and lift it aboard. This does not happen very often. There were times when we would make up to six good pickups in one day.

Some of the other war games consisted of having a torpedo attack either by plane or by ship. It was spectacular to watch the phosphorescent glow from a torpedo as it sped beneath the ocean surface, while the ship was trying to out-maneuver it. There were also the dive-bombers when the anti-aircraft guns came into play. Again the ship did a lot of maneuvering. It tried to make itself as difficult a target as possible. There were also the high horizontal bombers, with the ship doing as much maneuvering as it possibly could. There were fire drills, collision drills, man over-board drills, and abandon ship drills.

In the spring of 1941, Admiral Husband E. Kimmel relieved Admiral James O. Richardson as Commander-in-Chief of the US Pacific Fleet. Shortly after Kimmel took over as Commander-in-Chief, he moved the flag from the Pennsy to the Submarine base. When they say they are moving the flag, one thinks of five or ten men. Actually it is closer to 200 men, and all of the records go with them.

Throughout the spring, summer, and fall whenever the Pennsy and the Arizona were in port together, Roger and I would go on liberty together. We always had a good time. One time we were in Honolulu and we stopped at a restaurant, and I ordered rabbit, Roger said, "You have been all over the island, did you see any place where they raised rabbits?" I said, "No." He asked, "Did you ever see any wild ones?" I said, "No." He said, "What do you think they are going to feed you?" I said, "Rabbit." He responded, "Hell no, it will be alley cat, they have a lot of them here." Well, I ate it that night, but it was several years before I ordered rabbit again.

One Sunday morning we met at the front gate and took a bus to Waikiki to see the movie "Gone with the Wind," but the line of people waiting to get in was so long that we gave it up as a lost cause. So we went to the Royal Hawaiian Hotel and looked around the grounds.

There was another hotel on the beach called the Moana, it was the oldest on the beach, but not as nice as the Royal Hawaiian. After leaving there, we decided to walk back to Honolulu, which is a distance of three miles. By this time it was afternoon, and we were getting thirsty, so whenever we came to a bar we would stop and have a rum and coke. Actually we stopped at several bars, and by the time we got into Honolulu, we had more than enough to drink. That was really the first time that I had ever drank any hard liquor. It sure was good and it went down so easily. We got back to the Black Cat bar and restaurant and had something to eat, but that didn't sober me up one bit.

The Black Cat Café is one place that every service man wanted to go to at least once while in Honolulu. It was kind of a rough place, but you could get a meal at a reasonable price.

SAMPLING OF ITEMS FROM THE 1941 MENU OF BLACK CAT CAFÉ HONOLULU, HAWAII

Breakfast Dishes
Hot Cakes---$ .10
Waffle---.15
Oatmeal--.15
Corn Flakes--.15
Ham, Bacon or Sausage & Eggs, Buttered Toast and Hash Browns--------------------------.35
Poached eggs on toast-----------------------------.30
Egg & tomato scramble--------------------------.30
Oyster omelette-------------------------------------.45
Hard, boiled egg, pickled egg, or raw egg----.05

24 Hour Specials
Breaded Veal Cutlets---------------------------$ .35
Roast Turkey with dressing--------------------.50
½ Fried Chicken with Bacon-------------------.60
Roast Pork & applesauce-----------------------.40
Swiss Steak & brown gravy--------------------.25
Corned Beef & cabbage-------------------------.30

Spaghetti & meatballs---------------------------.25
Hot Pork or Beef sandwich---------------------.25

Steaks, chops and other meats
Porterhouse & mushrooms------------------$1.00
(most expensive item on the menu)
T-Bone---.60
Rib steak--.40
Hamburger   .30 with onions-----------------.35
Liver & onions   .30 with bacon-------------.35

Fish & Sea Foods
½ doz. Fresh Frozen Oysters, fried,
stewed or raw-----------------------------------$ .35
Fried Shrimps on toast-------------------------.35
Fried Ulua, Tarter Sauce----------------------.30

Salads
Fruit salad with whipped cream-------------$ .25
Crab --.50
Shrimp--.35
Potato---.15
Alligator Pear (avacado)----------------------.10

Cold Meats with Potato Salad
Boiled Ham ---------------------------------$ .35
Assorted cold cuts -----------------------------.35
Pig's foot ---------------------------------.20
Sardines ----------------------------------.25

Soups
Chicken -----------------------------------.20
Corn chowder ------------------------------.20
Vegetable ---------------------------------.20
Turtle-------------------------------------.20

Sandwiches
(Any sandwich under .20--on toast
.05 extra) Potato salad with
any sandwich .10

Black Cat Special-----------------------------$ .20
Bacon & Egg-------------------------------.20
Cold Ham----------------------------------.10
Bacon & Tomato-----------------------------.20
Hamburger---------------------------------.15
Hamburger & cheese---------------------------.20
Peanut Butter------------------------------.10
Club House--------------------------------.50

Denver---.25
Barbecued Beef------------------------------------.15
Hot dog---.10

Desserts
Strawberry shortcake with
    Whipped cream-------------------------------$ .20
Pies (per cut)--.10
Pie a la mode---------------------------------------.15
Brown bobbies------------------------------2 for .05
Ice cream--.10
Banana Split--.25

Drinks
Buttermilk ---------------------------------------$ .10
Milk (second glass .05) --------------------------.10
Postum---.10
Ovaltine ---.10
Milk Shakes --.15
Malted Milks --------------------------------------.20
Coca Cola & other sodas----------------------.10
    with meals .05

It was in the Black Cat the first time I ever saw two women fighting. They were using their fist, pulling hair and kicking. One was a waitress, the other was a customer. It seems that they knew each other. We didn't know who won as we had to leave in order to catch the bus back to the front gate, as our liberty was up at midnight.

We went across to the road to the YMCA and caught a bus back to the Navy base. I was in worse shape than Roger was, so he took me back to my ship. I ended up on the third deck;

I was so sick I thought I was going to die. On the second day, I was wishing I could die. My first class bos'n mate came down to see how I was, and suggested that I get to my quarters the next morning, which I did. There aren't many petty officers that would go as far as he did for a seaman. Joe Bennett was his name.

At one time he was the light heavyweight boxing champion of the fleet.

He had been in the Navy about fourteen years. Joe slept on a cot on top of a hatch cover that was not used at night; I slept directly above him in my hammock. When I would get into my hammock and I happened to bump his cot, he didn't say much, but in the mornings it was a different story. When reveille sounded, Joe would turn over and go back to sleep. The master of arms would come along with his billy-club and start beating on his cot and that, of course, would awaken Joe and he would get in an argument with him. While those two argued, I would lash up my hammock and get it stored and put away. Maybe that was the reason Joe was so easy on me when I got plastered. Joe was a tough leader, but if one did what he told him to do, every thing was okay.

One afternoon I rated liberty, and I didn't make up my mind until late to go ashore. As I was getting ready, Tom Gibson

, A coxswain, who had about six years in the Navy, asked what I was going to do ashore? I said I was going to get a tattoo. He looked at me rather hard and said, "like hell, do you want to be a walking comic strip?" I said, "well you have some tattoos," his reply was, "yes, and I'm a walking comic strip." I left the ship thinking about what he said, and I still don't have any tattoos.

When the ship was in port, they preferred that everyone get involved in some kind of sport, such as baseball, softball, basketball, boxing, tennis, or wrestling, however, no one had to join if he didn't want to. I decided to go out for boxing, not on the ship's team, but on the division's team, these guys played the rough way. They might not know much about boxing, but they sure knew how to fight. The first night we fought there were only two of us from our division that won, so we were eliminated. Before I joined the Navy, I did a little boxing in Detroit in the Golden Gloves and the Diamond Belt. In the Navy, we didn't have anyone for a trainer, there was no one to tell us how to fight, and I was used to being coached, such as staying in closer, or circling to the left or to the right etc. That was my first and last fight in the Navy, they were too rough.

While in port, the enlisted men had liberty every fourth day, and they had to be back aboard by midnight. The night I had duty, there was plenty of time to study for the next rate. In August I had six months in rate, which was a requirement for advancement. Then I became a seaman 1st class, and the pay increased to $54.00 per month. I thought to myself, I've lived on $21.00 for four months, and on $36.00 for six months, so why not send my increase home to a savings account. However, I thought if I did that, what would be the sense of making higher rates. Instead I decided to send half of the increase home, and keep the other half, and I did that every time I made a higher rate.

In September of 1941, the Pennsy came back to California and we dropped anchor at Long Beach. I got a leave for 13 days and went home, I really enjoyed that. My leave was up on the second of October, and the ship left for Hawaii on the third, We went to sea for the next fifteen days and were still in training and having war games. By this time my watch was on the foremast with the 50 caliber machine guns. We had four hours on as lookouts, and eight hours off. In the daytime when we had our eight hours off, we would be at our cleaning station working. I became a gunner's mate striker, which meant that I would be working with guns, cleaning them, and doing repairs. I no longer had to swab the decks or wash paint. I remained in the 6B division, and was still working with guns and ammunition. I had joined the Navy to learn a trade in order to be qualified to earn a living in civilian life. Perhaps this would come later as I still had five years to go in the Navy.

There were church services every Sunday morning on the fantail while we were in port. At sea they might be held some other place.

I don't want anyone to feel sorry for me for the way we had to live, or for the meals we had to eat, so I am enclosing copies of our menus for July 4, 1941 and for Thanksgiving of 1941.

OUTSIDE MENU JULY 4, 1941

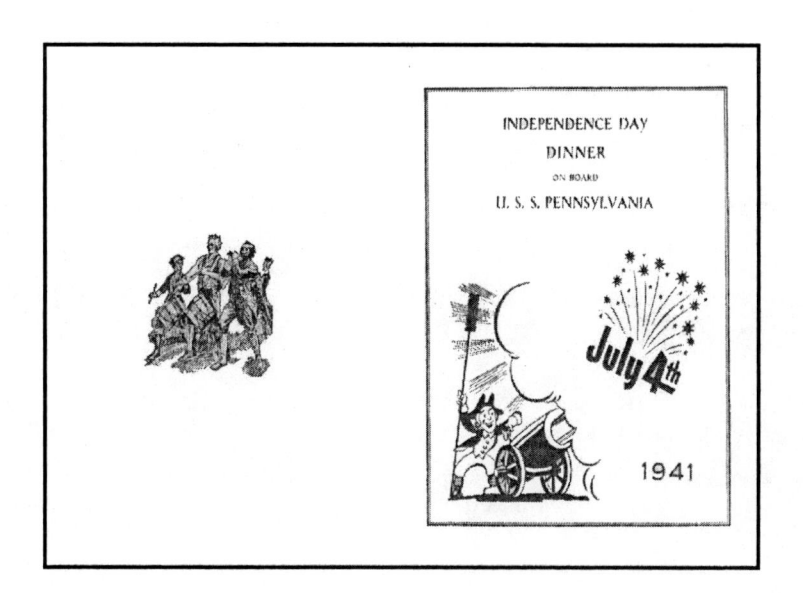

INSIDE MENU

U.S.S. PENNSYLVANIA   FOURTH OF JULY MENU
——— ———

Captain C. M. Cooke, Jr.   TURKEY SOUP
Commanding

———   CRACKERS

Commander C. F. Holden   SWEET PICKLES   RIPE OLIVES
Executive Officer

———   ROAST YOUNG TURKEY

Commander C. H. Gillian (SC)   GIBLET GRAVEY   SOUTHERN DRESSING
Supply Officer

———   CREAM WHIPPEDPOTATOES   BUTTERED PEAS

         CRANBERRY SAUCE

PARKER HOUSE ROLLS   BUTTER

ICE CREAM   APPLE PIE

         LEMONADE

OUTSIDE MENU THANKSGIVING 1941

THANKSGIVING

NOVEMBER
TWENTIETH
NINETEEN
FORTY-ONE
★ ★ ★ ★

U.S.S. PENNSYLVANIA

INSIDE MENU THANKSGIVING 1941

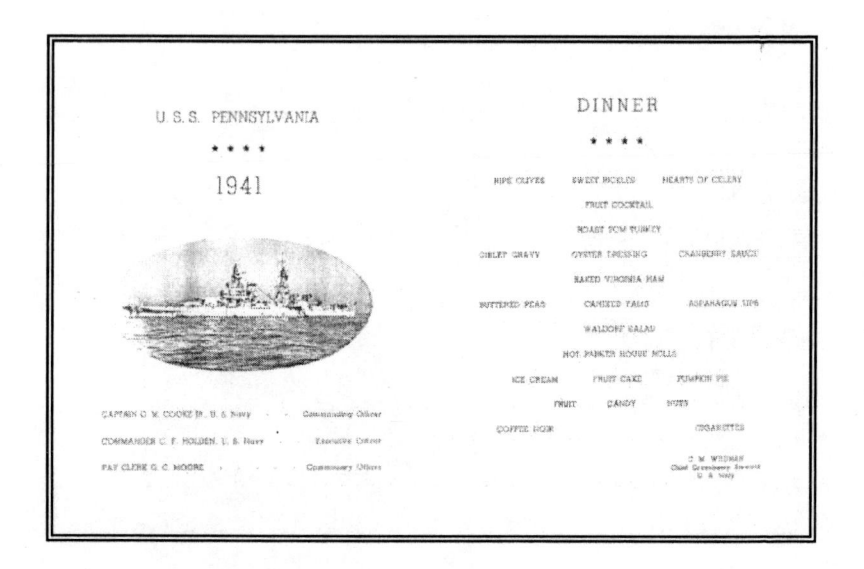

We also had a great Christmas meal in 1940.

There were a lot of us boots that came aboard ship about the same time, so we had a lot in common and that made us feel closer. The two fellows that I ran around with the most were James King and D.K. VanCourt. We went on a lot of liberties together.

   One day, either in late October or early November, we were standing an Admiral inspection on Saturday morning, when general quarters sounded, this was the first time that we ever went to general quarters during inspection. We never did learn the reason for it. I had gone to a 50-caliber gunnery school about the 15th of November, which was a ten-day school. I did real well, so I decided to stay as a gunner's mate striker.

   One day we were in the gunners' mate shop drinking coffee before we went to work. Spike Hennesey was there; he was the 1st class gunners' mate of the 6b division. Winsette was pouring coffee and he told Spike to say when he had enough coffee. Instead of saying "when", he said, that's enough, Winsette kept pouring, "Stop", Winsette kept pouring. By now the coffee was running over the top and it was burning his hands. He finally hollered "When!" Winsette knew he shouldn't stay around so he threw the coffeepot on the workbench and took off running for other parts of the ship. He came back on the third day after Spike had cooled down.

On the third day of December, we went into drydock #1.

It had been almost a year since the ship had had the paint chipped and been repainted under the water line. It had to have the barnacles scraped off the bottom and the screws. This is a job for the side cleaners.

59

A drydock has four sides where the back doors can be opened or closed. Bringing a ship in is very difficult; it takes several hours to accomplish this feat. Once the ship is in, the back doors are closed, the water is pumped out and the ship settles down on the keel blocks that were pre-set. Now the workmen can walk under the ship to work and they can keep dry. While in drydock, the ship gets it's utilities, such as water, electricity, steam, etc. from the dock. The heads aboard ship are not in use while the ship is in drydock so we had to use the ones on the dock.

DECEMBER 7, 1941

December 7, 1941, started just like any other Sunday in Hawaii. I slept in until just about 0700, which was later than usual. Roger and I had arranged to meet at the main gate at 1000 hours as we both rated liberty. I have never eaten much breakfast, and this day I drank only a couple cups of coffee, then went over to the dock to go to the head, take a shower, and shave. When I was coming out of the head, the first call to colors sounded, that is always at 0755 hours. About that same time I heard some airplanes diving, I looked up and saw something fall out of the first plane. I kept watching until the plane pulled out of the dive. I didn't see anything fall from the second plane, but I saw something falling from the third and fourth planes. Then I heard the bombs exploding. I couldn't see the target from where I was, but I knew something was wrong. I ran aboard ship on the portside and then over to the starboard side. Before I got there, I could see the target. It was Ford Island, the Navy airfield. It looked like the entire island was on fire. I don't know how many planes dropped their bombs from the time I started to run aboard ship until I got on the starboard side. I looked up and it seemed like they were coming from as far as I could see. About that time air defense sounded. I would estimate that from the time I heard the first plane to the time that air defense sounded would be about two or three minutes. We could see the Rising Sun Emblem, and we knew that we were under attack from Japan.

When air defense sounded, everyone who was connected with anti-air craft ran for their battle stations. Mine was down in #3 magazine with the 3-inch ammunition. This is located in the first compartment below the third deck. There are four rounds of ammunition in one box. We would put it into a hoist and send it up to the handling room, which is near the gun that fires it.

Shortly after air defense sounded, general quarters also sounded, so everybody would be at their battle station. All watertight doors were closed and dogged down. If this had been a surface attack, instead of an air attack, general quarters would have sounded first.

You must realize that five minutes ago we were a peace time Navy, sitting in drydock. The gun covers were on the guns, the ammunition was locked up in the ready lockers, and the tools used for working on the guns were locked up. While some of the gun crew were taking off the gun covers, others went to the small arms locker to get the keys to unlock the ready lockers. A chief gunner's mate took the nozzle from a fire hose and used it as a hammer to break the locks on the ammunition ready lockers. This chief had been on the Panna, which was a US Gun boat in China, and Japan had sunk that in 1937. The Pennsy was one of the first ships to open fire. There were four of us in the magazine, operating two different hoist. Fisher and I were operating #3 hoist, and the other two were on #4. We were sending ammunition up as fast as the handling room needed it. Then we started to have power failures from the dock, making it necessary to operate the hoist manually at times. Then we must have jammed it, because we couldn't operate it at all. So we started to carry it by hand. We were on the second deck just starting to go up the ladder to the main deck when a bomb hit and exploded. It knocked Fisher and me backwards down the ladder, and the ammunition fell on top of us. Some petty officer came along and told us to get back to our magazine and help the other two fellows get ammunition to #4 gun mount, as our gun was out of order.

The bomb exploded on the Pennsy at 0906. The time was recorded in the minutes of the ship's log. The attack lasted another forty minutes. We in the magazine did not realize when the attack was over, as we were busy sending ammunition up to the handling room until it was filled to capacity. It was close to 1030 before we got out of the magazine. As we were coming up the third deck from the magazine, we saw some fellows bringing down those who had been killed from the above decks. They were all bloody and very badly burned. They were being put in the brig temporarily. It almost made me sick.

Some of them were fellows that I had slept beside the night before.

From there we went topside. This is the first I had been topside since the attack started two and half-hours ago. We could not believe what we were seeing, every place we looked there was fire and smoke, in fact some of the blackest smoke one would see. We came out of the hatch on the port quarter as the bomb had hit on the starboard side and it was impassable. We looked down at the water and saw the fire on the Arizona,

and realized that this was where the black smoke was coming from. We looked around, and it seemed like every ship in the harbor was on fire, as well as everything on Ford Island. The hangers were burning, the planes were all blown up and still burning. Every battleship in the harbor was either sunk or damaged. Some were damaged more than others were. The Arizona, the California, and the West Virginia were sunk. The Maryland, the Pennsylvania, and the Tennessee were damaged. The Nevada was badly damaged, and the Oklahoma had capsized. The destroyers Cassin, Downes, Helm, and the Shaw were damaged.

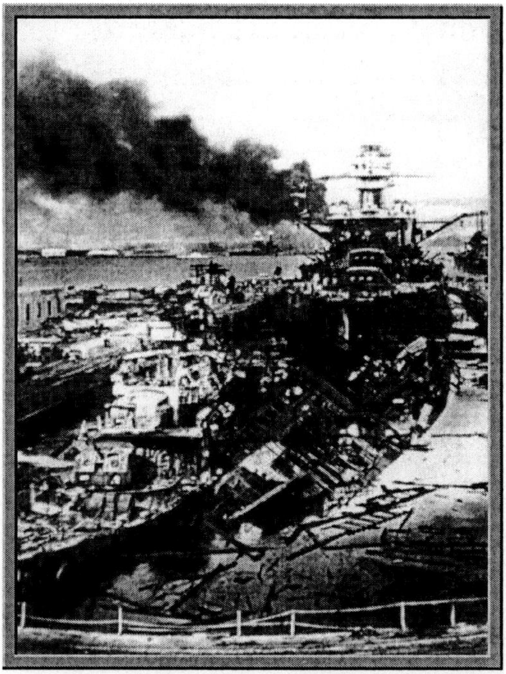

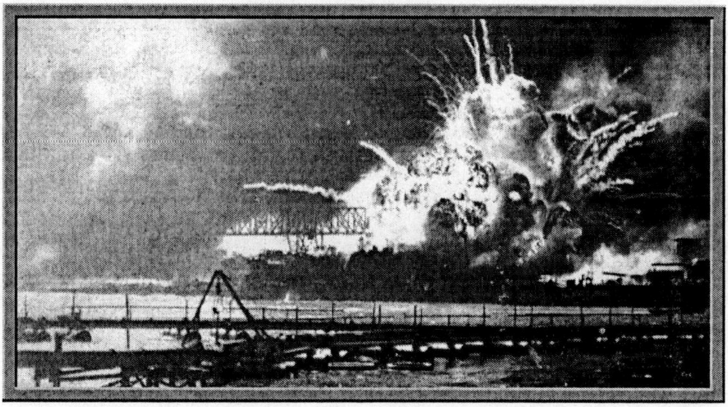

One minecraft, Oglala, three auxiliaries, the Curtis, Sotoyomo, and the Utah capsized.

All of the ships were eventually repaired and took part in the action later in the war. There was an oil slick all over the harbor that was coming from the damaged ships. Most of the ships that were losing oil had fire burning all around them. Navy personal was forced to abandon the more badly damaged ships as well as the ones that had capsized. This meant that men had to go over the side into the water that held the oil and was on fire, and then had to swim under water as far as they could come up for air, and do it all over again until they were clear of the fire. They either swam to Ford Island or to a whaleboat that picked them up. The coxswain of these boats got as close to the fire as they could. Some of them were pretty well scorched. The two destroyers sitting in the same drydock as us, the Cassin and the Downes, were hit by bombs, and one of them fell off it's keel blocks falling into the other one. When I came topside, they were both on fire and burning from one end to the other. The flames were so hot, and so close to the Pennsylvania that it started the paint burning on the bow.

By this time we were busy getting ready for the next attack that never came. We were taking care of the wounded, re-supplying our ammunition coming from the dock. We worked through the noon hour.

Some time around three o'clock they brought sandwiches to us. By this time there were all kinds of rumors going around and one of them was the Japanese were going to make a landing after dark. No one knew if there was any truth to this, but we had to be ready if it came; so some men from our ship went on patrol along the beaches with men from other ships. Nothing ever came of it. That night three of our planes flew over the harbor, and everyone was jittery as there was no way to identify them. I think every gun in the harbor opened fire on them. Two planes were shot down, the pilots coming out of them alive. After this, things quieted down for the night, but we were still at battle stations. This is when things got scary, when we had time to think. I was wondering what happened to Roger, was he down in the engine room doing his trade?

The next morning things looked a little brighter. Some of the ships had quit burning, and the mornings always make things look better. I asked permission from the officer of the deck to go ashore to see if I could find Roger, permission was denied. He said that maybe I could go later in the day or perhaps tomorrow morning while on a work detail. There was no way that I could get off the ship and look for Roger. Most of the survivors from the Arizona were topside sailors, and there were very few below deck sailors. I did not find anyone that even knew him. I wrote to my Dad and asked him to write to the Navy Department for information on Roger.

Royal Oak Sailor Gave Life in Attack on Pearl Harbor

Confirmation from the U. S. Navy department that Roger Joseph Bergin, fireman second class, was lost in action at Pearl Harbor on Dec. 7, 1941, has just been received by Charles DuBois, 1808 West Thirteen-Mile road. Both Alvin DuBois, son of Mr. and Mrs. Charles DuBois, and Bergin, son of Austin F. Bergin of Moose Jaw, Sask., Canada, enlisted in the Navy from Royal Oak in October, 1940. Because of a new job, DuBois enlisted two weeks later than his best friend and drew a different ship at the close of his training period.

Bergin was 24 years old. He was employed by Vogue Cleaners in 1937 and 1938, went to Ohio in 1939 and returned to Royal Oak in March, 1940, to enter the employ of the Model Cleaners. In Royal Oak, he made his home with the Howard W. McKinleys, 906 South Washington avenue. He was a motorcycle enthusiast.

Joining the Navy at $21 a month, Bergin advanced to a rank paying $60 a month in a little over a year.

He has two brothers in the Canadian Army.

ROGER JOSEPH BERGIN

71

For the next couple of weeks we worked along with the yard workmen to get the ship ready to sail.

The following is excerpts were taken from a Declassified document dated December 16, 1941 from Captain C.M. Cooke Jr., who was the Commanding Officer of the U.S.S. Pennsylvania, to The Commander-in-Chief, U.S. Pacific Fleet.

Hawaiian Area, December 16, 1941

1. Report of the action of December 7, of the times of attacks, of the number of planes involved, are based on conflicting and confused testimony of many observers, including the Commanding Officer, none of whom could observe more than a part of the action at any one time.

2. <u>STATUS AND CONDITION OF SHIP BEFORE ACTION</u>

In drydock No. 1 with three propeller shafts removed. Destroyers Cassin and Downes in dock ahead of Pennsylvania. Floating dock West of the new drydock occupied by destroyer Shaw. Cruiser Helena with Oglala alongside dock at berth B-s (Pennsylvania's normal berth). Pennsylvania had been excused from anti-aircraft drills while and because of being in drydock (no drills scheduled for Sunday). Machine guns in forecast were, however, manned. A Condition Watch of anti-aircraft personnel was available on board but not on guns. Commanding Officer and First Lieutenant were aboard, together with department representatives from each department; No orders to alert were received.

Ship was receiving steam, power, and water form the yard.

3. **NARRATIVE OF ACTION**

First call to colors had been sounded, about 0757; explosions were heard on the end of Ford Island abreast drydock No.1. When second explosion took place, it was realized that an air raid was in progress. Men started proceeding to their stations and "Air Defense" was sounded. Shortly after, general quarters was sounded. Condition YOKE was set as soon as stations were manned. In many cases men knocked off locks of ammunition ready boxes and ready storage's, not waiting for keys. 0802-attack by torpedo planes came in from the

West and the South, attacking the Oglala and the Helena and battleships across the channel. Number of planes not recorded, estimate 12 or 15.

0802 to 0805 (Exact time not known). PENNSYLVANIA commenced firing at the enemy planes, - reported as the first ship to open fire by personal on board. All anti-aircraft batteries were rapidly brought into action. After release of torpedoes three planes came in low from the port beam, straffing PENNSYLVANIA, straffing attack not effective. During the torpedo attack, one enemy plane was observed to burst into flames about 2,000 yards on the starboard bow.

Dive bombing attacks, torpedo attack on Pearl Harbor and dive-bombing attacks on Hickam Field continued.

Some time between 0800 and 0830, the NEVADA was observed to be getting underway and had reached a point about on the PENNSYLVANIA's starboard quarter, distance about 600 yards when a dive bombing attack was observed to be approaching the PENNSYLVANIA's on the port bow, 10 or 15 planes coming in succession, low altitude. This was between 0830 and 0900. This attack apparently was directed at the PENNSYLVANIA and the two destroyers in drydock. These attacking planes were taken under heavy fire. Just before reaching the PENNSYLVANIA, about two-thirds appeared to swerve to the left, a number of them dropping bombs at the NEVADA, with some misses ahead, misses astern, and at least one hit apparently in the vicinity of the bridge. The NEVADA was observed to stop.

At the same time, other planes of this attack passed to port and over the PENNSYLVANIA and dropped bombs, which fell in the water beyond the caisson. Except, probably for machine gun bullets it is believed that the PENNSYLVANIA was not hit during the attack.

One of the dive-bombers dropped a bomb on the SHAW in the floating drydock, setting it on fire.

DURING THE PERIOD 0830 TO 0915, HIGH BOMBING ATTACK.

The first attack coming in from ahead and passing to starboard is believed to have bombed the battleships across the channel.

The second attack coming in slightly on the port bow dropped bombs on the ships in the drydock, one heavy bomb hit the destroyer DOWNES in the dock ahead of the PENNSYLVANIA, one hit the dock approximately abreast frame 20 starboard of the PENNSYLVANIA a few feet aft of the 5"/25 gun no. 7, passing through the boat deck and detonating in the casemate of 5"/51 gun no. 9. The fifth bomb is believed to have struck the water outside the dock.

The bomb hits on the PENNSYLVANIA and the DOWNES occurred at 0906.

All high bombing attacks were fired on by all batteries. 5" bursts appeared to have been accurate, but later it was estimated that fuse settings were too short and that the bombing formation was not being reached, perhaps by several thousand feet.

FLOODING OF DRYDOCK

Flooding of drydock was started about 0920. At this time both destroyers ahead were heavily on fire. The bomb hit on the dock at 0907 had cut yard power; subsequently power on the ship for lights, gun operation, etc., were taken from the ship's storage batteries.

At 1010 the dock had become sufficiently flooded. Fire and bilge pumps on the ship were started, and at 1023 power on the ship was taken on two generators.

FIRE IN THE DOCK

Both destroyers ahead were on fire from stem to stern, and fire was transmitted to oil on the water in dock, setting fire to the paint on the starboard bow of the PENNSYLVANIA.

Fire was being fought by hose from the dock, on the side of the CASSIN. No hose was available for fighting fire on the DOWNES.

About 0930, explosions on the destroyers ahead began to take place, and at 0941, war heads on the DOWNES exploded on the starboard side, covering the area with debris. A section of Torpedo tube, weighing between 500 and 1,000 lbs. struck on the PENNSYLVANIA's forecastle. Precautionary measures were taken on the bow of the PENNSYLVANIA to prevent the spread of the fire internally. Fire was brought under control before serious damage resulted.

The Cassin, from which part of the bottom of the hull had been removed for dock work, rolled over on the Downes during the fire.

DAMAGE TO PENNSYLVANIA

A 500-lb. bomb dropped from high altitude bomber, 10,000 to 12,000 feet, penetrated the boat deck inside the protective shield and just above No. 7, 5"/25 cal. gun. After passing through this deck, apparently it was either deflected or rolled slightly in the compartment before detonating. The detonation caused the boat deck to open for a space of about 20' x20', opening upward, and the casemate deck was opened up in a similar area, opening up downward. The bulkhead above gun No. 9, 5'/51 cal. was blown out, and gun was put out of action. Explosion wrecked a considerable part of galley equipment and caused fuel oil from the service tank to run into the decks below. The explosion blast and fragments dished in the main deck and penetrated to the second deck. Three inch ammunition was being passed through the compartment on the main deck just forward of three inch clipping room, serving No. 3, 3"/50 cal. gun on quarter deck. At the time of the explosion, boxes containing about 24 rounds of 3" were in this compartment. Of these, cartridge cases of 8-3" projectiles were perforated, the fragments causing the propellant powder to burn, but none exploded.

 This bomb explosion caused fire in the casemate and on the main deck and on the second deck. Fire was difficult to put out because of the lack of pressure on fire mains, and because of difficulty of extinguishing fire in the painted cork lining on bulkheads. Fire, water and oil caused damage to officer's rooms on second deck in vicinity of explosion.

Casing of ammunition hoist to 5"/25 battery was dished in by the explosion putting this ammunition hoist out of action for the time being. Three flights of the hoist were also buckled.

CASUALTIES

The bomb exploded in casemate No. 9 caused the death of 26 men and two officers.

Of the men, a number were killed on gun No. 7, a larger number in casemate No. 9, and some additional in the "V" division compartment on the main deck under casemate No. 9, and some in the vicinity of No. 3, 3" gun.

Total number of wounded was 29. Nature of the wounds- severe burns, multiple wounds.

DISTINGUISHED CONDUCT

The conduct of all officers and men was of the highest order. There was no flinching. There was no necessity of urging men to action.

There were, however, a number of cases of wounded men insisting on continuing on station, serving guns, until ordered to battle dressing stations to have the wounds attended.

A number of yard workmen assisted in handling lines, fighting fires and one even joined the ammunition group of a gun's crew.

REPAIRS

Preparatory work for repairing damage of bomb hit was started by the ship's force about 1400. Later the following day, this work was carried on by yard forces and ship's force together. One 5"/51 gun and mount was obtained by ship's force from THE WEST VIRGINIA for installation on this ship [END OF DOCUMENT EXCERPTS].

Everyone was cooperative, and if someone needed help, all they had to do was ask. Everyone was willing to help the other fellow. I have never seen cooperation as we had aboard ship at that time. The uniform of the day on December 7th was shorts and T-shirts. If anyone was near a bomb when it exploded, the fire from the explosion would flash burn a person wherever the skin was bare. We had fellows that had second and third degree burns over forty percent of their body. I believe that most of our wounded were fellows who had severe burns. Shortly after that, there were no shorts or T-shirts worn as the uniform of the day. It would not be difficult to visualize how busy the sick bay was aboard ship.

Another thing that happened was that the fellows did not have earplugs or even cotton to put into their ears, when they got to their guns and started to fire. The guns that were firing over their heads would burst their eardrums. One of the worst cases was George Woodward. He was on a 3" gun, and a 5" gun was firing over his head all through the attack. When the attack was over he couldn't hear a thing. In a couple of days when his ears stopped bleeding, he got a little of his hearing back. When I left the ship a year and a half later, he still didn't have all of his hearing. There were a number of minor casualties where the fellows didn't go to sick bay after the attack. There were so many who were a lot worse off, and the doctors had their hands full. I was one of those who waited. When I was knocked down backwards, and the ammunition fell on me, it hurt my back. When I did go down, and I told the doctor what happened, his reply was, "Now that there is a war on, are you trying to get out of the Navy?" That hurt my feelings, as I have never run away from a fight even as a kid. I left the sick bay, and was never in it again as long as I was aboard that ship.

By December 17th the ship was ready to get under way, but we didn't leave until the 20th, as we were being pulled away from the dock by the tugs to get us into the channel. The ships all around us were cheering and waving, and some even stood at attention. They thought the same as we did, that we were headed to sea to hunt the Japanese fleet and make a fight of it.

We aboard ship, for the first two days out, had no idea that we were headed back to the states. On the 23rd of December, we did meet a Russian cargo ship heading west. We were at sea on Christmas day, and we were in a storm. I had a watch from midnight to four in the morning as a look out. My station was in the foremast with the 50-cal. machine guns. We were very disappointed when we found out that we were state side bound. We went to San Francisco to finish being repaired and to get some newer type guns. The new guns were a 1.1 pom pom. They were made by the British, and they were a rapid firing gun. They replaced the 3" gun.

  The first two weeks in Frisco were great. We were one of the first ships back from Pearl Harbor, and when we went on liberty, we had identification on our uniforms indicating that we were at Pearl on December 7th. When we went on liberty, our money wasn't any good. The civilians would pay for our meals, buy our drinks, and we never knew any of them. We would be walking down the street and some man or woman would say, "Sailor, can I buy you a drink?" We did have a few drunk sailors aboard ship.

While in Frisco, there were alot of men being transferred from the ship; they needed men with experience on new ships that were coming into the fleet. They were being replaced by men coming out of boot camp. Aboard the larger ships, there are always transfers going off and on.

In January or February of 1942, we put out to sea having no idea where we were going. While at sea there was always lot of training going on. One could bet that whenever we were at sea there would be one of three things that we would doing, working, standing watch, or training. We finally pulled into Pearl and stayed there for a while. We left there and on March 23rd we entered San Francisco Bay.

In April, Captain Cook left the Pennsy, and Captain King took Command. Since the war started, we never knew where we were going. There were always a lot of rumors, and once in awhile they were right, but not too often. We were under way the middle of April, and there were lots of rumors as to where we were headed. The task force included seven battleships and six destroyers. The sea was very rough, with high winds. Some men got hurt on the forecastle as the water was coming over no. 2 gun turret, One plane crashed in landing, but was salvaged. The next day it was still very rough, and we lost another plane while landing. So far we had seen nothing on this cruise, Around the twentieth of April we must have gone south, as it became quite hot. The sea calmed down, and we refueled two destroyers. The next day we started to use salt water for showers. The sea got rough again and the Colorado lost a plane in landing. This cruise took place because of the Coral Sea Battle; we missed it, and returned to Long Beach on May tenth.

While in Long Beach I had enough time in rate to take the test for 3rd class gunner's mate. There were probably 200 fellows taking tests that day for advancement in rates. Winsette, sitting across from me asked what are the two gases; up to that point it was very noisy in there, just as I whispered Persistent and Non-Persistent the compartment became real quiet and my voice throughout the compartment. The officer in charge walked behind me, picked up the test papers, and reached over and picked up Winsette's papers and said, "You two fellows can come back in three months to take the examination again." In other words he kicked us out.

We went back to sea, and returned to San Francisco about the 29th of May, We fired all our guns. Shortly after we had tied up, we started to take on stores. On the first of June we heard that Tokyo was bombed for the first time. On June 3rd, the Japs attacked Dutch Harbor and Midway.

On June 5 1942, we got under way with four battleships, one carrier, and a pair of destroyers. The next day we met two more battleships and two more destroyers. It was announced today that the Japs were met at Midway and repulsed, and now our fleet is in pursuit, we may see action this time. Around the tenth of June a heavy fog came in and caught our aircraft in the air, the pilots were told to land near any battleship they could find, and not to try to get back to their own ship.

The Pennsy picked up five aircraft that day. The Colorado had one plane crash into it killing the crew. Again, we did not see any action. We saw enemy planes, but they were out of range of our guns. We pulled into Pearl Harbor in July.

I was quite faithful about writing home. When I came back to Pearl, I would always write that I had seen Roger today, that way my parents would know that I was in Pearl and not out in the war zone, so they wouldn't worry too much. I think I forgot to tell you that immediately after the war started, all of our out-going mail was censored, and we couldn't tell anyone where we were or where we had been.

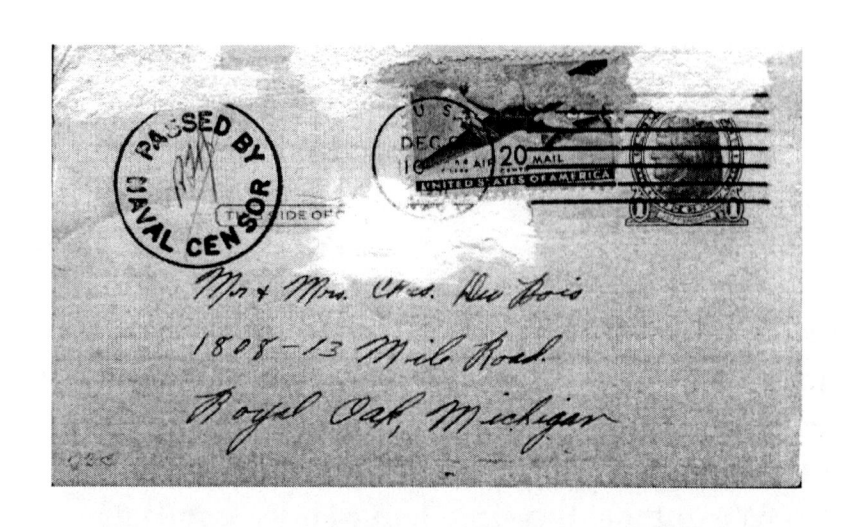

Mr. & Mrs. Chas. Du Bois
1808 - 13 Mile Road
Royal Oak, Michigan

NOTHING is to be written on this side except to fill in the data specified. Sentences not required should be crossed out. IF ANYTHING ELSE IS ADDED THE POSTCARD WILL BE DESTROYED.

I am well ~~(sick~~ ~~(serious~~
~~I have been admitted to hospital as (wounded (not serious~~
~~Am getting on well. Hope to return to duty soon.~~

I have received your (Letter dated Dec. 3, 1941
~~(Telegram dated~~
~~(Parcel dated~~

Letter follows at first opportunity.
I have received no letter from you (for a long time
. (lately

Signature Alvin E. Du Bois
Date Dec. 9, 1941

Some time in September 1942, we pulled into San Francisco for a major overhaul. We were moved off the ship, and we lived in a warehouse that was on the same pier that the ship was tied up to. That way we were right there to go to work every morning, and at the same time we were not in the way of the yard workmen who were working on the ship. Between the yard workers and the crew they were changing the appearance of the ship, and at the same time was making it more efficient.

We got a thirty-day leave so we could go home if we wanted to. Fisher didn't have money for train fare, so I loaned him a hundred dollars. He said he would pay it back as soon as he came off leave. Well he never did go home on leave. He spent his thirty days in Sacramento, and was broke when he came back. I did get my money from him, just before I was transferred from the ship in the Aleutians.

They took off the after mast, replaced it with a shorter and wider mast which housed the range finders and the after-control center. They replaced all of the 5" guns, the 25, the 51 caliber, and the 1.1 pom pom that was never very successful, and the 50-caliber machine gun. The 5" was replaced by the 5" 38 caliber; it is an anti-aircraft gun with a much longer range. It can also be used as a broadside gun, and these are twin mounts. The pom pom was replaced with quads 40mm. They were a much better gun. The new 20 mm, replaced the machine guns, this gave us a much greater anti-aircraft defense, some of these guns were new to the fleet and even the gunners mates had to be trained on them. We had to go to school to learn how to fire them, and also how to fix them if something went wrong.

 While in Frisco, I also went to a deep-sea diving school. There were different reasons for wanting this school. One-- after you qualified you received $20.00 a month more in your pay. Two--you had to be a qualified diver in order to get a warrant gunners' commission. My first dive was in Long Beach California. It was beautiful down there. The bottom was sandy and very hard; you could walk all over. You could see all kinds of fish. I only went down to ninety feet that day. The second dive was at

Puget Sound in Bremerton Washington. The bottom there was all murky. When your feet hit the bottom they would sink about another six inches. You could hardly see your hand in front of your face. I went down looking for two pistols that were dropped overboard. As luck would have it, I started to feel my way around in the muck, and in five minutes I found them. From there another diver and myself went to inspect the screws on the ship. I also made a dive in San Francisco Bay. A merchant ship was loading some ammunition and the net they were using broke and dropped about fifteen boxes in the bay. They asked of us to come over and see if we could find them. So two of us went down, and the other six fellows stayed up on topside to handle our lines. After about an hour they signaled for us to come up. We had only found four boxes at this time, but we knew the location of the others. When we got on topside it was time for noon lunch. We went to their dining area and they gave us menu to order from, we had never seen that before in the Navy, and that food was real good. The eight of us decided that maybe we should eat supper there. We could if didn't send up the rest of the ammunition too soon. We ate supper there.

    Deep-Sea Diving is real hard work but it was fun. The suit you put on, your helmet, the shoes, and the weights weigh close to a hundred pounds.

After you get all your weights on your helmet is the last thing to go on. You do not dare put your helmet on before you get into the water, because you can't see good enough where to place your feet with the helmet on. You also have to be careful that you don't' miss your footing. You do not want to go down to the bottom without your helmet on, because if you do your gonna drown. Now actually, you don't drown as much as the pressure at the bottom of the ocean is so great against your suit that it squeezes your whole body up into your helmet, and naturally it kills you. When you go over the side there's always three men to help you over, and your head stays above the platform until your helmet is on. Your air comes into the helmet and is controlled with a valve on the left side, but you use your right hand to control that valve. To get the right amount of air to your suit you extend your arm to your side and get the arm where it will merely float. You don't want it to go up in the air, you don't want it to fall down the side you want it just to float. When you get the pressure regulated there then you are ready to go to down. But as you go down, this is why your right hand is on the value, because you must give yourself more air so that the pressure underneath will not squeeze you into the helmet. It sounds complicated but it's no place near as complicated. After you make the first, second, third dive, you get use to it. The main thing is don't fall off anything before you get your helmet on. This is the main thing, and always there are two to three guys helping you with your footing, because you do not have good balance carrying all that weight with those big shoes.

Now once your on the bottom and you see something, say the bottom of a ship up there maybe five, ten, fifteen feet, and you want to get to that ship for some reason; the way to do that is to turn on your air, so that air will make you float, so that you can get up to the height you want. Once you get there, then you have a check-valve inside your helmet that you grab with your lips, but most of us have to use our teeth in order to have strength enough to open that check-valve to let some of the pressure out. Otherwise you float right back up to the top, and if you did this, then your suit would split open. If your suit splits open you would fall right back down to the bottom. It sounds alot more complicated than what it is, but it's something you do pay attention to.

We got a new gunnery officer abroad. He is

in charge of all the ordinance of the ship. The air defense officer asked the new gunnery officer if he wanted somebody to explain the operation and repairs of the 20mm. I was cleaning a 20mm at the time, so I got elected. I was to explain to him all I could. But I knew I didn't do a very good job, so I said to him, If you want more information get Pappy Lyons, he can explain it much better than I can. He said to me, "Young man, you did a very good job. I understand the gun very well." I knew he didn't, because I didn't know enough to explain it to him.

Inside living quarters they did away with the sleeping hammocks, they replaced them with either cots or bunk beds; I got a bunk bed in the gunner's shack. We were in Frisco for a long time; I made a lot of liberties and had a wonderful time. Cecil King and I used to go to college football games on Saturdays, and pro-football games on Sunday. In the fall of the year it gets cold and windy, so one Sunday we got a bottle to keep us warm. This one Sunday two women sat in front of us. Everytime a good play was going to happen, they would jump up in front of us and we would miss that play. In a Navy uniform you don't have any pockets, so I put the bottle in the waistband in front. When the next good play came along, the four of us jumped up. The bottle came out of the waistband, fell on the cement, and broke. The women did not care for odor so they changed seats. If they would have only changed seats in the first place we wouldn't have been so cold. Cecil didn't forgive me for that for a long time.

I used to get off at Market Street and the waterfront, and make my liberty at the neighborhood bars. There were not many sailors, and I got to know the people that visited there quite well, I have a few stories I could tell about that town, and some of the screwballs abroad ship.

This one is about a gunners mate named Cook. He liked the size of a 40mm shell casing, and he thought it would make a pretty lamp. He had to disarm it and everything want good till he got down to the primer. He couldn't figure out how to explode it. He finally ended up using a punch, a pair of pliers, and a hammer. When he went to explode it the rest of us gunners' mate left the shack. After the small explosion we went back to see what happened. He had powder burns on his left hand and split two fingers and his thumb. This is the story he told the doctor; "He was lighting a cigarette when a book a matched caught fire and burnt his hand. On the way down to sick bay a hatch fell on his fingers and split them open". The doctor accepted his excuse. You never explode ammunition abroad ship, accept in an authorized place.

In February of 1943, we finally got under way and went to Long Beach for more training, over 50 percent of our crew were boots, and even the experienced men needed practice on the new equipment. One night we had a night air defense practice, and we fired the 20mm guns. There was a group of 20mm just outside of Admiral Pye's quarters. It was George Woodward's cleaning station, so he had to clean the guns before he could hit the sack. It was about 10:00pm., and he had the midnight to 4:00 A.M. watch. He wasn't happy. At this time I was standing a watch just a little ways from where Woodward was working, so I went over to talk to him. The conversation was going something like this. "Anybody in their right mind wouldn't be firing this time of night, and what enemy would have a night air raid?" I saw Admiral coming, but he was too close for me to tell Woodward, so I stepped on his hand, and all he did was move it, and kept on talking. I finally kicked his arm, and he told me to quit kicking him. By this time the Admiral was standing over him, as Woodward was on his hands and knees on the deck working on the gun. Even though it was dark, he knew those shoes and pants were not mine. He jumped to his feet and saluted. The Admiral said, " Sometimes it is a tough life, isn't it boys," and walked away. Woodward gave me heck for not telling him that the Admiral was coming.

In May of 1943, we got under way for parts unknown. After we were at sea for three days they issued us cold weather clothing, including parkas insulated pants, boots, and mittens. The following day we were told that we were on our way to the Aleutian Islands, which most of us had never heard of, let alone knew where they were, they are west of the Bering sea.

Every morning at daybreak we were at general quarters. Just before securing, we would test-fire all guns in order to give us practice on the way they worked. One morning they told the 40mm gun captains to load six rounds in each breach, they come four rounds to a clip, that meant we had to split two clips; so I thought it would be easier to put two clips in the breech and have each gunner count the rounds that were fired, and when his gun fired six rounds, to put the gun on safe and no more rounds would fire. The idea was good, but no one knew that once the firing key was held open that the gun could not be put on safe. After the firing, each gun captain had to report how many rounds were fired from each gun, there were four guns to each mount, all the gun captains reported a maximum of four rounds per gun except one, he had anywhere from four to six rounds per gun. Sky control wanted to know why his guns fired so many rounds, so he was called up to explain. When he got to sky control, there were at least ten officers that wanted to hear how he did it, this same gun captain had made 2nd class gunners mate about a month before. All the big wheels from the gunnery department were there, he went from one to the other to explain what he had done, every one of them asked the same question, "Don't you like your rate?" We can't have a 2nd class petty officer that can't follow orders. I finally got down to my division officer, he looked at me and said, "DuBois, there just isn't anything else that hasn't been said." I think the reason I got off so easy as I did, is that probably no one else aboard ship knew that it wasn't possible to put that type of a gun on safe when the firing key was held open.

The reason for this cruise was to make the invasion of Attu. Attu is the farthest island west in the Aleutian Island group, we were getting close to Japan at this point, it seemed like it took us a long time to get there. The sea was very rough and it was cold. The ship was bobbing like a little ball in a lake, and it seemed like every wave was coming over the bow with the water running the full length of the ship. It was cold, and although we had our parkas, insulated pants, boots and mittens on, we just couldn't get warm. We were standing watches of four hours on and four hours off, twenty-four hours a day. The waves came over the ship so much that the salt spray was getting on the guns and we had to put covers on them. We also had to keep covers on our ready ammunition at the guns for the same reason. On our four hours off in he daytime, we had to do minimal maintenance on the guns to keep them in firing condition.

At this time I am the leading gunner's mate of the tenth division and I was supposed to know what was going on in this division. Word came down from sky control that the ammunition covers were not in place on gun mount #12, as the waves were taking them off. They sent two men down to secure them. These men were to have life jackets and lifelines on. So VanCourt, the second leading gunner's mate and I started to do the job. We were on the quarter-deck when we heard the wave hit the bow of the ship, and we knew it was going to come right on over us. By this time I had my lifeline tied, but VanCourt didn't. So I tried to get to him. The wave hit and lifted VanCourt up over the ammunition shield, and set him down straddling it. It knocked me down, and started to wash me overboard. My stomach hit a stanchion, and when I ended up, my head was overboard on one side of the stanchion, and my feet on the other side. Some of the fellows that were on lookout saw the wave hit us, and reported two men overboard. They never thought that we would still be aboard ship. This was another time when I came very close to losing my life. They said the water was so cold there, that fifteen minutes is all that a person could live in it.

    We arrived in the Aleutians the early part of June, and it was light until one or two o'clock in the morning. This was hard to get used to. We started to bombard on the tenth of June. The landing for the army was scheduled for the next day. The landing was good, and they established a beachhead right away. I sure felt sorry for those fellows, as they had to get in that cold water and wade ashore. The Japs put up a fight for a few days, but some of them would sneak down into the mess line of the U.S troops and get their chow.

I don't know of anyone that liked Attu, including the Japs.

The sea had been rough ever since we arrived there. About the seventeenth, the gasoline blew up in the bow of the ship, so we had to return to the states. We put in at Bremerton, Washington for repairs. Bremerton was a good Navy town they liked to see the ships, and we always had a good time there.

VanCourt made second class gunner's mate at this time, so they put him on the port watch and left me on the starboard watch. That meant that we could not go on liberty together. They assigned us to shore patrol duty on opposite days from one another. No one like this duty but someone had to do it.

The second time I was on duty, a full Commander and his wife were walking toward me shortly after I had gone on duty. They stopped, and the Commander said there was a sailor crapped out in the middle of the sidewalk about two blocks back, and ordered me to get him out of there. I went back there, and sure enough, he was there. I shook him and finally got him to talk. I asked him what ship he was from, and he replied that it was none of my ----- business. I asked him if he was staying in a hotel, and again he replied that it was none of my ------- business. I told him that I would have to take him in, unless he would tell me the name of the ship or the name of the hotel. Again he told me that it was none of my ---------- business. So I started to take him to shore patrol head quarters. On the way we came to an alley. He said, "Turn in here, it's a short cut." I didn't know if he wanted to take me down there and then try to make a break for it, or what he had in mind. I started down the alley, and got the billy-club ready to use just in case. A little way down the alley, we came to the back door of shore patrol headquarters, and we went in. The officer in charge asked what charges there were against him. I said, "None, just let him sleep it off." Five hours later at nine o'clock I was passing the alley, and there he was coming out. He didn't even know me.

Van had the duty this one night, and I was on liberty. I came out of a bar and looked up and down the street to see where I wanted to go. I saw a fight going on in the next block, so I just stayed there to watch it. I glanced up the other way, and I saw Van coming out of a bar. Checking on bars is part of our job. He looked toward the fight, and turned and walked the other way. The next morning I was teasing him about it and all he did was shrug his shoulders.

 We left Bremerton around the first part of August, and again was issued cold weather clothing. A couple days out we were again getting into rough weather. We were told that we were headed for Kiska, which is another island in the Aleutians. We bombarded for a couple of days before the invasion was made. The invasion went off very well, and the soldiers made good advances all day. That night about 2:00am., someone wearing earphones reported to sky control that there were tracer bullets flying overhead. A marine on a lookout station aboard ship reported this. No one on sky control could see it, so the officer in charge sent his assistant down to the lookout station to check this out. He told the marine that he couldn't see anything. The marine was

pointing at the ones flying overhead. Finally he said, "come on the other side of the ship, and I will show you where they are landing in the water." The assistant did this, and went back to control, and reported that he couldn't see anything. The sky control officer called group ten, which is on the fantail of the ship. He asked group ten if they could see any tracer bullets flying overhead. The replay was no, as the sun was in their eyes back there.
Everybody that had phones on took them off, and no one tried to make an issue of it. They took the marine off the lookout station, and put him in sick bay with another marine as a guard over him. The landing was advancing so fast, with no resistance, they then realized that there were no Japs on the island. They must have left the island before we had made the landing. We left there and went back to Adak, which was under US control.

    All there was in Adak was a place to drop anchor, some airplanes, airplane hangers, barracks, a dock, and a few trucks. While swinging around the anchor chain, the ship receives a request to transfer some different rated men. On this list they wanted two-second class gunners mates to go to Washington DC for advance gunnery school. VanCourt and I had been requesting transfers for the past year, but we never had gotten one. When they request certain rated men to be transferred, the department heads try to fill that request. It makes them look good. VanCourt got his transfer papers immediately, which filled one vacancy. Someone stopped the other one. The day they were to leave the ship, I was down in the gunnery office when the gunnery officer walked in. He said to the yeoman, "Who is the other gunners mate that is being transferred?" The yeoman answered, "I don't know, sir." The gunnery officer asked whether anyone was qualified. He replied, that DuBois is here, and has been requesting a transfer for over a year. He turned to me and asked if I wanted a transfer. I said, "Yes, sir." He told me to get my sea bag ready, as I had one hour before the boat was leaving the ship, and I was to be on it. He told the yeoman to get the release papers ready, and to help me get them signed. There were five different officers that had to sign them. Three of them were no problem, but the air defense officer, and my division officer were not going to sign at first. It was one of these officers (or maybe both) that had kept me aboard ship for the past year. I can't blame the division officer, as he would be losing both of his second class gunner's mates, and that is all he had. He would have to depend on his third class or have someone transferred from some other division if he could. The fellows down in my living Compartment packed my sea bag for me, and I was ready and waiting for the boat. There were about 30 men, all petty officers, but with different rates, being transferred that day. Most of us were going to different schools. Some were going to a receiving station for further assignment. All of us had volunteered for this transfer. I believe this is the first time I volunteered for anything, as once in a while it is the right thing to do, (I hope).

    We left in a whaleboat along with our sea bag and hammock. It was even rough going to the pier. We had to throw our sea bags and hammocks, which are tied together, up on the dock. One machinist mate was a well-built man, but he had a difficult time getting his sea bag and hammock on the dock. From there we put them on a truck with two men throwing them on. The truck took us to the barracks. We slept on cots that night, and the next morning the truck picked us up and took us to the plane that was flying us out. That same fellow was having a hard time with his sea bag and hammock. We landed in Anchorage that afternoon, and went through the same procedures as we did on Adak.

Anchorage, Alaska was warmer and not nearly as windy as it was in the Aleutians. Shortly after we were there, we asked when we were going to get air transportation out. They told us that it would be at least three weeks if your name had not been taken off of the list, and then it would be longer. Why would our name be taken off the list? The response to that was that while we were there we would be working on construction, and most of us would out-rate the men that were in charge of the job. To get our names taken off of the list, we would have to give the man in charge a bad time. He would report this to the C.O., and our name would go to the bottom of the list. He told us that we would be working with a pick and shovel, and perhaps an air hammer. He also told us to do what we were told, and we would get out when our turn came up. One day while walking back to the barracks, I ran into the marine that saw the tracer bullets flying overhead. I knew him quite well as our cleaning stations were side by side. I called his name, and we talked for while. It was then that he told me what the score was. His wife was going to have a baby, and he wanted to be with her. The doctor aboard ship was sending him back to the states, to a hospital for observation. I told those silly so and so's I would be home to see my kid born. In fifteen days I was flying out. We were flying commercial airlines. There were all Navy people on the plane, so they left the cockpit door open, so we could talk to them. They had to make a landing in White Horse for refueling. Until then I always thought the co-pilot was as good as the pilot with the exception that he didn't have enough hours of flying time. The co-pilot was landing the plane when the wheels hit the runway.

I swear we bounced a hundred feet in the air. The pilot took over the controls and finished the landing.

We arrived in Seattle with no further incidents. On arrival, the sea bags were loaded onto trucks and taken to a pier, they were unloaded, and we carried them to a warehouse that had sleeping facilities, again I noticed the guy had trouble with his sea bag. Van and I were going to be there for five days before we would catch a train for DC. We didn't have much to do, so one day we did our laundry. As we were sitting on the cots folding our clothes, the fellow with the sea bag sat down on our cot and started talking. I finally asked him what in the world did he have in his sea bag that would make it so heavy. He said "Nothing!" Van and I looked at each other, and Van said to him, "Pick up DuBois' sea bag and hammock." He did, and he asked: "Where is the rest of your stuff?" I said, It's all there. He said, "It doesn't weigh half as much as mine." He went over to his sea bag and started to take everything out, about two thirds of the way down he came across a piece of railroad track about ten inches long, the thing must have weighed one hundred pounds. Of course, we all had a good laugh over that. Someone from his division put it in when he wasn't around.

Van and I had a lot o fun in Seattle; it was a lot nicer than taking the ferry back and forth to Bremerton. There was one place in Seattle where you couldn't buy booze, but you could bring you own bottle and buy the mix. They had dancing and a lot of girls but we were not there long enough to get acquainted, as we hadn't found the darned place until the night before we left for DC

The trip was uneventful; we got our sea bags off the train and carried them to a taxi, which took us to the navy yards. The driver took us to the front gate and let us off, as he couldn't go into the yards. The SP at the gate told us where to go, it was about three quarters of a mile, we asked him who was taking care of our sea bags, you guessed it, we were, so we carried the darn things to the barracks. It struck Van and I kind of funny. At Adak they had trucks that took our sea bags and at Anchorage they did the same thing.

At Seattle the trucks took them to the pier, in DC they didn't do anything for us, so it looked like the closer one gets to the Capitol the less service one gets.

We went to the master of arms office to report in, while we were talking to him, low and behold, who walks up but the master of arms that always fought with Joe Bennett about getting up in the morning. He inquired about different men from the ship, and if so, were they still aboard. The officer in charge said, as long as you know these fellows, you might as well take care of them, so he took very good care of us. When we thought we might be late coming off liberty, all we had to do was tell him in advance and he would clear us. We were on liberty about sixteen hours a day for a week before we had to report to the gunnery school.

We reported to gunnery school, and everyone was either a petty officer or a commissioned officer. There were better than two hundred and fifty in the class, it was a twelve-week school. We were to study one type of gun for a week, then go on to another type.

We would also study about ammunition and hydraulic systems. The class was divided into groups of twenty fellows; the officers had their groups the same as the enlisted men had theirs. When one group was being instructed on 40mm, another was on 5'/38 etc. The school was running twenty-four hours a day, one class every eight hours. Van and I got the midnight to eight in the morning shift those were great hours. We got out of class, went over to eat, then we went to the barracks and slept. We got up around three to do a little studying, then got ready for liberty. We would come back from liberty in time to change clothes and be in class by midnight. There were only two things wrong, we didn't dare drink too much, and we had to take our dates home early. Van and I were always short of money; it seemed like we were always writing home for some. It was our own money, but we knew were spending a lot. We had been saving for over two years and we were spending it like drunken sailors. In order to justify ourselves, one of us would say to the other, "How do we know that we will be around to spend it later?" The other one would say, "Oh what the hell, lets go out and have a good time."

The third week of class we were to study the 5"/38 gun mount plus the electric hydraulic system. This was going to be a three-week class. Our instructor was a 1st cgm, who had served aboard a destroyer in the north Atlantic. The ship was shot out from under him, he was missing a hand that was taken off just above the wrist, and he was still trying to get used to it. The very first day in class he put a cigarette in his mouth and started to reach for a match with the hook that replaced his right hand, well, nineteen matches were lit. The only reason that there weren't twenty was that I couldn't find mine. Instead of him lighting the cigarette, he took it out of his mouth with the hook, and told us when he needed help he would ask for it. You could have heard a pin drop, he was a good instructor, we really learned a lot from him.

Van and I did study; we studied mostly every afternoon plus the nights we stayed on base because we didn't have the money to go on liberty. I was always between the fifth and tenth place. We finished classes, and they gave us a three-day leave starting Monday morning. We saw our buddy, the master of arms and told him our problem, he said he would take care of it, although he threatened us with our lives if we screwed up or were picked up by the shore patrol, or if we were not back onetime. Everything was fine, until the Executive officer of the school wanted to see us Monday. Our buddy told him we had just left, but he would try and catch us if he wanted him to, the officer said that he would see us when we got back. We were still not off the hook, because we couldn't be in Detroit Saturday, when our leave didn't start until Monday morning. So this means that I had better not get into any trouble.

    I was on a train sitting in a seat minding my own business when a couple of shore patrol guys went by, one of them really looked me over. In a little while they came back and this one stopped and asked me if I was from Royal Oak, Michigan, I said I was, then he wanted to know if I recognized him, I said I didn't. Then he wanted to know if I ever rode motorcycle, I said I had. He wanted to know if I was riding with my brother when we both got stopped by a police officer and they gave us both a ticket? I said I did (one of nineteen tickets). He said, "Do you remember I said I wouldn't give you a ticket if it wasn't for the other fellow," I said "ya", I always wondered what my brother did that I didn't do." He said, "I didn't mean your brother, I meant the other cop," I said, "Boy am I glad that you told me, because I have been blaming my brother all these years." We did a lot of talking the rest of the trip. It was nice to get home and see Mom and Dad again, but it was too short of a visit. I returned Wednesday night so I would be there for muster the next morning. Van got in a couple of hours before me.

After muster Thursday morning, we went over to the executive officer's office and reported in. He seems like a pretty nice fellow. He asked if we would like to be gunnery instructors at Great Lakes Training Center that caught us by surprise. We thought we had to see him because he found out when we left the base to go on liberty. We just looked at each other, and finally we asked when we would start. He told us that we would have to go to instructors' school, and that wouldn't start for another week, and we could have a weeks leave if we wanted. After that the school would last for two weeks. We told him we would take it. He said that the reason he was offering this to us was because of our marks We left to go to the barracks to get ready to go on leave. This time it was legal. We both came back a day early and when we saw each other, we both said that we didn't want to be instructors, we wanted to go back to sea. So now we had to go see the executive officer. We walked into his office, and the first thing he said was, "How was leave?" We both told him fine, but we had a problem, he asked what it was, and we told him that we wanted to go back to sea. He sat there for a few minutes, his face getting red, finally he asked what kind of a ship did I want, I answered that I would like a destroyer. He turned to Van and asked him, Van said the same. (If looks could kill, we would have been dead.) He said, "You two fellows will get your destroyer, and you will get them damned quick, but they won't be the same ship." Two days later our names came out on the transfer list. When we received our orders, Van was assigned to the USS Robinson, DD562; I was assigned to the USS Ross, DD563. We didn't get the same ship, but we didn't expect to, but we did get sister ships and would probably be in the same squadron and travel together.

We received our travel orders, and the executive office must have forgiven us as he gave us ten day delayed orders. Van was supposed to go to Tacoma, Washington and I was to go to Treasure Island in San Francisco Bay. With delayed orders, I could spend about nine days at home, and still report to the receiving station on time. I forgot to mention the fact that Van and I made 1st cgm, when we were through school. When I left DC I boarded a train for Detroit. I was feeling very happy that I had made 1st class, which paid $84.00 a month. I was going home on leave, and it was all legal. After that I was going to California, and I was assigned to a new destroyer that hadn't even been put in commission. Every thing was going my way. I arrived in Detroit feeling cocky.

When I was in the lobby of the train station, a SP came over and asked for my leave papers. I said to him jokingly, "I don't know that I have to give you my leave papers." He said, " You do when I tell you to." My answer to him was, "let's see your ID, " He said, "I don't have to show you my ID card." By this time a crowd gathered around figuring some sailor was in trouble. I said, "If you don't show me your card, how do I know that you are even in the Navy?" He started to look for his card, and would you believe that he didn't have it. At this point I started to feel sorry for him. Then he asked, "Do think I would be out here if I didn't have to?" I said, "guess not, but I don't have any leave papers. I'm traveling under orders, with delayed orders." So I handed him my papers. He said, "fellow why didn't you do this in the first place?" I said, "I just wanted to see if you had your I. D. card." He said, "I won't be without it the second time." Then I caught the bus for Royal Oak.

When I arrived home my folks were surprised to see me, they hadn't expected to see me so soon. This time I called Mrs. Othout to find out about Pat. Pat answered the phone, and we made arrangements to go out and eat, he was bringing his wife along. Pat had been accepted into the Navy after the war started, and he went to the East Coast. He had a ship sunk out from under him, and was in a hospital for months, and was given a medical discharge.

I left Detroit to go to California; I had to change trains in Chicago. It was a lot different this time than it was three years ago when I was on my way to boot camp. I knew what I was doing. I went over to the ticket window to get a berth assigned to me, and the guy at the ticket window said he didn't have any berths. That meant that I would have to ride the day coach, I said my orders call for a berth. He replied that he didn't have any, I told him to give me back my orders, which he did. I left his window and was walking through the terminal looking for a SP, I didn't find one, but I did find an M.P. I asked him to do me a favor, he said he would if he could. I told him that the fellow at the ticket window was trying to give me a run-around, he said he would sure help. The two of us walked up to the ticket window, and I told the fellow at the ticket window to tell the M.P. what he had told me, because I was not leaving here until I got a berth, even if I had to stay a week. He replied that it wouldn't be necessary, as he just had a cancellation, and I could have a berth. If I had let him get away with this he would have charged the government for a berth, and would have sold it to someone else and pocketed the difference. One learns alot in three years about finding one's way around.

    I finally arrived at the receiving station on Treasure Island, and was assigned to a cot for the night. When I got to where the cot was, there were some other fellows there that had been assigned to the Ross. There were only a handful of us then. Two of them had been there for a week, but most of them had just arrived. The next morning we fell out for muster, and I drew a work detail; that night I went on liberty in San Francisco. I went back to some of my old haunts, saw a few people that

I knew and had a good time. Because of my rate, I didn't have to be back until 0800 in the morning. We mustered the next morning, and I drew another work detail; in fact I drew a work detail every morning for two weeks. I said to myself, "This is for the birds." I walked up to the petty officer in charge, and said to him, "You will want to hope that you don't ever get on the same ship that I am on, because I will make your life miserable." He asked, "Why?", I replied, "You have had me on work detail every day since I came here, and I out-rate you by two grades." I don't believe that I have pulled rate on anyone before. To be fair about this, we wore dungarees at the receiving station, and we didn't have our rates sewn on our shirts. He could not look at us and know, but it was on his muster sheet. After that, I didn't do any more work details at Treasure Island.

There were more fellows coming in every day who were assigned to the Ross. We finally had enough, so we could have one end of the barracks for just the Ross crew, and we had our own area where we fell out to muster. One morning we were at muster, and the executive officer came over and asked me a question. I could hardly talk. He wanted to know what was wrong. I said my tonsils were inflamed. He told me to go over to the hospital and have them taken out. I went to the hospital and talked to the doctor who told me I couldn't have the tonsils removed when they were so inflamed, I was back at the barracks for noon muster, and the executive officer said that he had told me to go to the hospital. I told him that I had, and I was told they couldn't operate as long as they were inflamed. He told me to come with him, and we went back to the hospital. The executive told the doctor that I was the only 1st cgm. assigned to the ship. We would be leaving in three weeks, and he wanted me to be ready to go. He sure did not want me sick at sea, as there wouldn't be any replacement out there. The doctor asked the commander to step into the office. So they went in and talked. When they came out the executive told me to get my toiletry and be at the hospital by 1700 hours, and they would operate the next morning. They did operate, and everything turned out well.

We left Treasure Island on the 9th of February 1944 to see our new ship in Tacoma, Washington. We traveled by train, and there were probably four or five carloads of us. Each car had a petty officer in charge. That night someone woke me to tell me that someone was going to get off the train in the next town. I went to the compartment where this sailor was. I just stood there and heard him ask a fellow to pass his handbag out of the window when the train stopped. It was dark in the compartment, and no one saw me. As the train stopped, I told the guy that "I would not do that if I were you." It surprised everyone, and they left and went back to their bunks.

I went over and talked to the man who wanted to get off. I told him there were no more stops until we arrived in Portland. He was to see me an hour before we would get in. The next morning he came back where I was. So we started talking. I told him we had a three-hour layover in Portland, and most of the fellows were getting off the train and going with their friends to see the town. I asked him what he wanted to do. He said he would like to go to town. I asked him how I could trust him to be back on time to catch the train. He promised to be back on time. I made a deal with him. I told him if I let him go he would have to promise to be here on time, and stay aboard the train until we get in Tacoma and muster. He promised. What he didn't know was that the only alternative I had was to have him stay with me. I didn't want that, as I had other plans. When the three hours were up, he was on the train, and he stayed on it until we were in Tacoma and mustered. I reported all my men were present. We got into trucks that took us to the barracks, and by the time we arrived there, he was gone. He had gone AWOL. However, he did live up to his promise to me.

USS ROSS (DD 563)

The next morning we went to the ship. She was a pretty sight, but she was small. The ship was being built by the Seattle-Tacoma Shipbuilding Yards. The yard workmen were putting the finishing touches on it. That day most of us just looked the ship over. Of course, I was interested in the gunnery, so that is where I spent my time. There were 5-5" 38, single barrel. 5-40 millimeter quad mounts, (4 guns to a mount), and 5 groups of 20 millimeter guns. There was a small arms locker that held handguns, rifles, machine guns, and line-throwing guns. There were magazines that held the ammunition, one for each 5" gun, plus the 40mm and the 20mm Ammunition. There was also an ammunition hoist in each 5" turret, plus the different ammunition ready boxes. This is the equipment that I would be concerned with.

The following day we fell out for muster in front of the barracks, and there were more fellows than just the ones that had come up from Treasure Island. We were divided into our own divisions. The torpedo men, fire control, and gunnery made up the ordinance department. I was in the gunnery division. This division fell in by itself so we would get to know one another. I met the chief gunners mate. I was the only 1st cgm assigned to the ship. That gave us a total of 18 rated men. The ship rates over 30. Seventy percent of them had never been to sea, and only three of us had ever seen action.

Sea-tac personnel took her out for the final trial run. We, the future crew, were invited to go along. It was the first and last time that I had a free ride on the Ross, (as none of the sailors had to work.) We were very proud of her. She performed wonderfully well. It was the fastest ride aboard ship that I ever had. I knew that I was going to like this duty, at least I thought I would.

The 21st of February 1944, was the day that the Ross was commissioned. There were 325

officers and other men who made up the crew; it was a cold, but a bright day. I can remember during the commissioning how cold it was. I looked around and there were a lot of us shivering. There was a letter read from the Secretary of the Navy saying that we wouldn't have a lot of time to get the ship ready before seeing action. The Captain, B. Coe, gave his talk. In his speech he told us to learn our jobs well, because our life, or the life of the man standing next to us might depend on it. All of us aboard ship are dependent on each other, and I'm sure none of us wanted the feeling of guilt when the man beside us is wounded, or dead, because we didn't know our job.

A destroyer is so named because that is its duty, namely to destroy. It is designed to torpedo other ships, to drop mines on submarines, to shoot down aircraft, to bombard shore installations, to lay down smoke screens, and protect other ships. It took us about three weeks to get familiar with our part of the ship. The first time we went out to fire all of the guns I goofed. I worked along side of the chief to get the 5" ready to fire, not paying enough attention to the rest of the guns. All the 5" but one fired O.K. Only one 40mm fired right. I never asked the chief what they said to him, but they sure chewed me out. I started to tear down the guns to find out what went wrong. I found that most of them had too much grease in the chamber which would not let the gun recoil like it should, so they jammed, you can be assured that the next time every gun on the ship was ready.

On March 10th, we got under way for San Diego, as we would get more training there. On the way down quite a few of the fellows had gotten seasick. It was a much rougher ride than one would get on a battleship. The ship traveled at 20 knots, and made the trip in five days. The very next day we started our training. A lot of men aboard ship had to learn in two months what I had learned in one year, plus learning anti-submarine warfare, submarine evasive action, line handling, and the rigging of paravanes. Our training involved other ships including battleships, aircraft carriers, submarines, and other destroyers. There was trouble with one engine during one of the exercises and we came into port late that afternoon. We also fired the 5" guns that day. Anytime the guns were fired they were to be cleaned as soon as possible. We were coming into port, and all the gunners' mates were on topside working on the guns in their work clothes. I went below deck for something, and when I came back, I couldn't find a gunners mate, I was burning. Someone told me that the master-of-arms had kicked them off the topside because we were coming into port, and they had to be in the uniform of the day. I found the master-of-arms, and he confirmed it. I didn't ask who gave the order, I assumed that it had been the executive officer, and I knew he was on the bridge. I told him that half of the gunners mates rated liberty just like everybody else, and I thought they should be allowed to go, but I wanted the guns cleaned first, and I couldn't see why they couldn't clean them on the way into port. As I started to say something else, he said, "DuBois, get off the bridge, and stay off until you are sent for. That is a direct order, so you had better do it." As I was walking off the bridge, the first class signalman said, "You screwed up this time. It was the Captain who gave the order." The Captain stood beside the executive, and didn't say a word.

I believe that the Captain stood by to see how the situation was going to be handled. He wanted to see how the executive was going to handle it, and what my reaction was going to be. At that time the ship was very short of petty officers. We were a new crew, and had been together for only a month. That was the last I heard of it.

One of the new crew members was Smoky, probably one of the best cooks in the Navy. We both went aboard the USS Ross at the same time. He always said, "You might not eat to good at sea, but when we get into port, where we can get fresh food, we will make up for it." He was sure right. One evening we were going on the beach together, he said, "Wait a minute, I want to go through the chow line". He asked the mess cook what was leftover. He said, tomatoes, onions, and gravy. Smokey said, "Save it, if you want you can dump it all together". At this point I said, "What the hell are you going to feed us". His answer was, "That's your cream of tomato soup for tomorrow.", and it was good. At that time, the cook was allowed fifty-four cents per day, per man, for rations. That is why he used leftovers whenever he could. We really ate good abroad ship when we were in port. When in port, we generally had fresh fruit most anytime we wanted it. It was left in the open so you could help yourself.

About the middle of April, we left San Diego for Puget Sound. On the way up our shakedown was complete, and we were ready to join the fleet. We still had to do the normal drills such as: abandon ship, man overboard, fire drills, and collision. We anchored in the bay. For the next couple of weeks we took on supplies, fuel, and water. Each department checked their equipment and made necessary repairs. We left port on the 30th of April. There were a few guys that missed the ship when we sailed. A couple of them caught up with us at Pearl Harbor. I guess the others were deserters. One of the guys that came aboard at Pearl was the one that wanted off the train on our way to Tacoma.

We were with three battleships, and four destroyers. Each ship while at sea or in hostile waters goes to general quarters long before dawn. We arrived in Pearl on the 10th of May 1944. It had been over a year since I had been there. They sure had been busy cleaning up. Of all the ships that were sunk, damaged, or capsized on December 7th, they were all repaired and back in action, except the following: Arizona, Oklahoma, and the old target-towing ship, the Utah. It was a lot nicer coming back there than it was on December 8th, 1941.

Underway from Pearl on our way to Eniwetok, we arrived about June 7, 1944. Eniwetok covers a large area. There was a lot of coral reefs, but very little land. It looked like the ships were at anchor in the middle of the ocean. We were there to assemble the task force that was going to make the attack on Saipan and Tinian. The 15th of June was the target date.

A new officer came aboard. He was assigned to the gunnery division as an assistant division officer. He was just out of college and this was his first assignment. He was all right, but some of the gunners' mates were taking advantage of him. I let it go for a couple of weeks then one morning after we had muster, I took him aside and told him that when he gave an order, it was to be obeyed. The men were not to ask why. If they did, and they will, I told him his answer to them would be, I told you to and then to drop it. I'm sure he didn't like an enlisted man telling him how he should handle things, but later on he found life was easier for him.

    On the 11th of June, we were underway for Saipan, with four light carriers and five destroyers, the destroyers being the screen for the carriers. The airplanes from the carriers were to furnish anti-submarine protection and air cover. We were to give protection against enemy sub, surface, and air attack against the carriers. We were warned that these waters were being controlled by the enemy, and we were warned to keep a sharp lookout at all times.

On the 15th of June 1944, the invasion of Saipan started on time. Our carrier planes began to bomb the beaches and the airfields. They were given air cover from early morning to dark. We did not see any action, but we were in constant danger. One night we had a man go overboard, it was a bright moonlight night, the kind that invites air raids. This was a decision the captain had to make, and these are the facts. We were in enemy held waters, as part of a screen for four aircraft carriers. There was a bright moon with attacks possible, and it was known that there were enemy subs in the area, the Ross would have to come to a complete stop to pick up the man, and we would be very vulnerable to either air attacks or submarine torpedoes. He gave the order to drop out of formation and try to pick up this man. They had plotted his position the instant he went overboard. The ship turned around to that position, but could not find him. At last someone heard him, but still could not find him, the captain gave the order to turn on the searchlights, this was done, and they found him immediately and we were underway.

The Captain had risked his ship and 324 lives to pick up a man that he knew was alive in the ocean. There was something strange about the whole thing, before he jumped, he had put on his life jacket, wrapped tape around his watch, and put a whistle around his neck. It was obvious that he had planned to go overboard, but his plans didn't go any farther, he was a very lucky man to be found and picked up. When he saw the captain, he admitted that he was only fifteen yeas old. The captain put him in the brig for safe keeping until he could get him transferred back to Pearl. Who do you think the man was? He was the same man that wanted to get off the train going to Tacoma, and he had gone AWOL before we got to the barracks, he had met the ship in Pearl on our way here. Perhaps if I had handled the problem differently on the train, this incident would not have happened.

     Even at sea in the middle of the ocean there were always rumors, the rumors went that the marines were having a difficult time making a foothold, and were losing a lot of men. Marine General Smith was having too many casualties under his command, so he was relieved of his command, and replaced by another General Smith. Even aboard ship one wonders how these rumors get started.

Day and night we were with the aircraft carriers as their screen. One day there was a torpedo wake on our starboard side, another destroyer was dispatched to go after it, and we were to stay in our position on the screen.

One evening when the planes from the aircraft carriers were returning to their ships after bombing the beaches, the Japs followed them back, and our radar didn't pick them up until they were almost back. Our planes were almost out of gas so they had to try land. We could not fire at the enemy for fear of hitting our own planes. Some of them landed safely, but a few went over the side, we would mark the spot where they crashed and would try to pick them out of the water. We picked up two pilots, and it was getting dark when we tried to find the third one, the captain cut the engines so we might hear him if he hollered. Someone on the bow heard him, but we couldn't locate him, again the captain turned on the searchlights, found him and got him aboard. I never saw a man so appreciative; we were his last chance for that night. In the morning, someone might have found him, but the odds were against it. It was always a great satisfaction to everyone when we picked someone out of the drink. We succeeded in rescuing every man we went after except one; he crashed landed, and we were there in minutes, we found him, but he went under the water as soon as we arrived. A man from the ship dove overboard, but could not bring him up, we were all very sad over that. We had been to sea so long that we needed to refuel, we pulled along side of a tanker while we were under way, everything went well, just like the book said it would.

We made some runs back to Eniwetok escorting carriers, after ward meeting other carriers and escorting them back to Saipan. For the next two weeks we continued to operate as before, giving air support to the ships, and to the marines and army ashore.

On the ninth of July, we headed back to Eniwetok with two other destroyers. We had a week for fueling, repairs and replenishment of supplies. By this time the crew had gotten to know each other pretty well. My chief gunners mate, Murphy, was about five years older than I and was as nice a fellow that one could meet. He always called me kid. One day he said, "I want you to know the Blue Jacket Manual better than anyone else on this ship." I asked, "Why?" He responded, "Some day it might do you some good." The Blue Jacket Manual was the "Bible" for seaman in the Navy. I believe it kept me out of trouble. I knew just how far I could push things before I had to back down, and there were certainly times that I had to back down. There were times when we had a lot of fun. We were sitting in Eniwetok where we were beginning to consider it as safe. After 1600 hours (4:00pm), we didn't have a watch and could do whatever we wanted, most of us would take showers, put on clean clothes and go down to the mess hall to eat. After chow we would come on topside and stand around and tell stories (lies) to each other.

    The water was clean and blue, and it was great for swimming, except that it was salt water. One day when I was standing with Vernon and Rosengren, I said that when Ferrell comes by let's grab him, take off his watch and his shoes and throw him overboard with his clothes on. Ferrell was no small guy, but neither was Vernon or Rosengren. We thought it would be fun, so we did it. Everyone involved had fun, including Ferrell. The next night we did the same thing. Ferrell took it good-naturedly, but the third night we tried it, Ferrell had help. He had my chief, and he had Vernon's chief and those two guys were BIG! They almost put us over the side.

    No one was allowed to drink alcohol aboard ship, but when the captain thought the men were up tight, he would have a liberty party on the beach, and each man could get two beers, that happened while we were in Eniwetok. Of course there are always some who do not drink, and they would give it to someone who does. Our assistant division officer came aboard and looked me up; it was obvious that he was angry. He said, "DuBois, when so and so comes aboard restrict him to the ship for two weeks." I asked, "Why?" He answered, "Because I told you to." That made me mad. I said, "Sir, you don't have the authority to restrict him nor do I." He said "You either restrict him, or he will get a summary court martial." My reply was, "He is restricted to the ship." This is the time to back down. When the gunners mate came back aboard, I found out what happened, the sailor had gotten drunk, pulled out his gun and threatened to shoot him, so actually he was letting him off easy. The irony of the whole thing was, two days after the incident; we were under way, so the restricting didn't mean a thing. We were headed south. Two days before we were to cross the equator, they told us when we would be crossing it.

 Crossing the equator is quite a ritual in the Navy. It depends at what point the crossing is made, and how safe it is in wartime. It also depends on the captain of the ship. We had a good captain. I think, he figured that it would be a good time for the crew to let off some steam that had built up in them.

 A "pollywog" is a person who has never crossed the equator, at least by his records. A "shellback" is a person who has crossed the equator, and it is recorded in his records. I believe there were only two 1st class petty officers that were pollywogs, Timmons, first class signalman, and I. the day before crossing is "pollywog day". The day of the crossing is "shellback day". Tim and I were pretty well liked, so we felt that the shellbacks would give us a rough time on the crossing. Now this is all in fun. So we got a lot of the pollywogs together and planned our attack. We decided to give haircuts, making a plus sign on top of their heads, also using the fire hose to wash their clothes while they were wearing them. Now these guys just didn't let us do these things without putting up a struggle, but about seventy per cent of these sailors hadn't been to sea until they had come on the Ross. Of course, they couldn't be shellbacks. So we did have the upper hand. After a few of us got it started, the rest of the pollywogs took action. I was standing on the searchlight platform resting when an egg just missed my head. The captain went into the galley, got some eggs, and I knew that it was the captain who had just missed my head. He went back to get more, but the chief cook wouldn't let him have any more. Our executive officer wasn't too well liked, so some of the pollywogs gave him a hair cut. He wanted to make an issue of it, and I guess the captain talked him out of it. The shellbacks were being manhandled that day.

The compartment that I slept in had only about eight bunks, and we were either 1st class or 2nd class petty officers. When I was ready for bed, I went to the compartment, and no one was down there. I thought, that's strange, because generally I'm not the first one to go to bed. I had the midnight to four o'clock watch, so I went to sleep. At midnight when I was called for the watch, only about half the bunks were filled. I went on watch and asked some of my crew if they had seen any of the fellows from the sleeping compartment. One of them said that he saw a couple of them go down to the sail-maker locker. Then I thought that these guys are up to no good. My whole crew that night, were pollywogs, so I told them to be prepared for anything tomorrow because we had, had our fun today. The next morning after breakfast, the shellbacks started to serve subpoenas on the lieutenants and the leaders of the pollywog for mutiny.

My specific charges were as follows:

Charge I--DuBois, A. E. now a GM1c U.S. Navy has hitherto willfully and maliciously failed to show reverence and allegiance to our ROYAL PERSON, and is therein and thereby a vile landlubber and pollywog.

Charge II--Mutiny: Leader of pollywog against shellbacks.

Charge III-- Being a U. S. O. Battleship pollywog.

Disobey this Summons Under Pain of our Swift and Terrible Displeasure. Our Vigilance is very Wakeful, Our Vengeance is just and Sure.
        Given under our hand and seal
        Attest, for the King
        DAVY JONES
        NEPTUNUS REX

The reason that no one was down to their

bunks last night as that they were getting things ready for today. They had gone through this on other ships that they had been on, so they knew more of what they were trying to do. They took pieces of canvas about thirty inches long and about six inches wide, sewed the width together to make a tube, they sewed one end closed an filled it with sand, then they sewed the other end closed. They put that in salt water to soak overnight. Now they had a real paddle. I don't know how many they made, but it seemed like every shellback had one. They also made a tube about thirty feet long, and it was open on each end.

    They took the lieutenants and the leaders of the mutineers, then the rest of the pollywogs. We had to take all of our clothes except our under shorts, then they sprayed us with salt water from the fire hose. There were two columns of men, and we walked between them and they used their paddles on our butts, if we went through too fast, they made us do it over, this time on our hands and knees. From there we went to King Neptune. The charges were read against us, and he passed sentence. I was sent to **NEPTUNUN REX** barber shop for a hair cut, also to his dentist. The hair cut wasn't bad, it took about six weeks to grow out. **NEPTUNUS REX** dentist was something different, they checked the teeth for cavities, didn't find any on anyone, but we all had bad breath, so they brushed our teeth with liquid black shoe polish and quinine mixed. They took us over to this 30-foot long tube, it was filled with garbage, and they must have saved it for a week. They had salt water running in one end very slowly, so as not to wash the garbage out of the tube, but just to make it nice and juicy. We had to get into the other end and crawl through all that garbage. As we were crawling, some wise guy would step on top of the canvas and our heads would bump into his foot, they would say, "Get a move on", and down would come the paddle on the butt. This happened five or six times before we came out the other end. Only Tim and I were given the next ritual. They put a potato on the deck near #1 gun turret, the deck slopes upward and we are on our hands and knees. We had to push the potato to the bow of the ship with our nose, if the potato rolled backwards more than three times, they would use the paddle on us. Try pushing a potato up hill with your nose! We were now shellbacks, and we received a certificate to prove it. Tim and I had welts on our behinds for a week afterwards. Everyone had a good time, and it did relieve some of the tension.

We were told that we were on our way to Espiritu Santo, just south of the Solomons. We had two weeks of peace and quite. We got underway the 24th of August with three aircraft carriers and two destroyers. One of the destroyers was the USS Robinson. In three days we were anchored in the harbor off Manus, we knew something was in the wind, but we didn't know what it was.

Then one day the chief gunners mate went ashore and ran into an old buddy. Murphy asked him what was coming up, and he said the invasion of Pelews. Murphy then wanted to know if the Ross was going to be in it, and he said it was, it seemed like everyone on the beach knew where we were going except us. That made Murphy mad, so when he got back aboard ship, he was telling everyone where we were going. Finally the captain sent for him, and he wanted to know where he got his information, Murphy said it was common knowledge on the beach. We were underway two days after that conversation. The captain opened up his orders and we were headed for Peleliu. I didn't see Van while we were on Manus, but hoped to in the next port. On our way to Peleliu we refueled from the port side of the USS Idaho. The following day at dawn we were off the beachhead of Peleliu, close ashore to give fire support for the Under Water Demolition teams. The hazardous work of the UDT's was first daylight reconnaissance of landing areas in the war. Our job was to hammer enemy machine gun emplacements, pillbox, trenches, sniper hideouts, and spotters, using our five-inch batteries and our 40mm machine guns, We were to come in as close to the beach as we could without running aground. The UDT finished its survey for that day without any casualties.

For the next two days we were back in furnishing fire support to the "frogmen'. They worked at clearing out boulders, coral, reefs, and wooden obstacles, blasting them out of the way to clear channels for the landing craft, and the landing ships to the beach. When we would see a flash from one of their guns, that was our signal to open fire on that flash. There were other destroyers, cruisers, and battleships, all bombarding the Island. It was the largest bombardment to date in the pacific.

Besides the daylight bombardment, we were harassing the Japs with night illumination. It didn't give the defenders much time for rest or sleep. The frogmen were all volunteers. They had to be very athletic and great swimmers. A PT boat would get within a short distance of the beach, and the frogmen would go over the side rapidly, carrying a pack on their backs. The pack contained explosives to blow up the coral reefs and to get other obstacles out of the way for the landing. The PT boats never stopped to pick up the men. They had a loop mounted on the side of the boat that looked like an old tire. The men would put their arm through that, and it would throw the men aboard.

On September 15th, 1944, the troops started to land. Every gun in the bombardment group let go with everything it had followed by aerial bombs and rockets. The more troops we were landing, the more gunfire came from the enemy, and it was coming in with more accuracy. A signalman on the bridge of our ship looking through a pair of glasses saw a movement in a palm tree. He decided it must be their spotter. We opened fire with a 5"gun. The first round was short, the second round was right. We got return fire. Our third round brought down the tree. Up to this point Chief Murphy and I were sitting on an ammunition ready box watching what was going on and drinking coffee. When that first round from the enemy came as close as it did, we left our coffee cups and took cover. Murphy thought the cups might get broken, so he went back after them, so we had two rescued cups. I mention this just to show what foolish things a person does when one is excited. Murphy and I were at our battle stations when this incident happened. We were on ordinance repair. We could be around any gun as long as the phones were connected to central control. We did not have a job to do unless a gun broke down, then it was up to us to get it back into commission as soon as possible. The enemy had our range, but thank goodness, we were a moving target. The shells were falling all around us. The director-operator spotted gun flashes on the hill, and all the 5" guns went to automatic, meaning the director-controlled the guns. The Gunnery officer ordered all guns to shoot. Meanwhile, enemy shells were splashing around us, the ship was maneuvering. The order was to give hard left rudder with full speed ahead. About that time our gunners thought they had eliminated the guns that we were firing at, and we did not receive any more shells. For the next six days we furnished fire support for the marines ashore, and at night we furnished illumination with starshells and harassing fire, to wear down the enemy.

 We shot up a lot of our ammunition, and about the 20th of September 1944, our orders were to take Ulithi; taking on ammunition from a merchant ship in route. We pulled along side of the ammunition ship on a Sunday morning, and we were to take on as much 5" and 40 mm ammunition as we could handle in an hour's time. That was our allotted time for being along side the ship. The enemy still had submarines in these waters. The merchant marines refused to load us, as they did not get paid for working on Sunday. The captain of the merchant ship allowed us to send men over on their ship to handle their equipment, and the ammunition. It took a lot of time to get the men over there, and to handle the ammunition. We only picked up about half of what we should have. When we pulled away we headed for Ulithi. Fortunately the Japanese left the atoll just before we arrived. We of course, didn't know it at the time, so we bombarded for a short time. One of the spotters saw some natives waving and jumping up and down. Ulithi atoll became a central point of Naval Operations, almost like Eniwetok. We were back at Peleliu around the 26th. The marines were suffering heavy casualties. The first week they had 3,946.

On September 30, 1944, we got underway to go back to Manus. It was a quick trip as there was a lot of work to do before the coming battle. We had to get resupplied with oil, ammunition, provisions, and other supplies. We knew that whatever was coming up it was going to be big. There were all kinds of ships at anchor. On the 10th, fifteen or twenty small ships left. They were either tugs or minesweepers. We left on the 12th on our way to Leyte Gulf. We were the bombardment and fire Support Group. About the 16th, we met three oil tankers, and started to get fuel from them. While fueling the wind became very strong and the ocean was running high. Before we finished we had problems staying alongside, yet being careful not to get too close to the tanker where we might collide, or too faraway that the fuel hose would pull apart. We finally were fueled and we pulled away. The storm was getting worse by the hour. While we were fueling, other ships were fueling from the other tankers. The job did get completed as scheduled. During the night the storm did not let up a bit. The next morning at daylight it seemed like it was getting worse. The waves were getting higher and higher, the swells were enormous, beating against the bow and the spray coming over the ship. There were strict orders that no one could be on topside without a life jacket and a lifeline on. Because of what had happened to me in the Aleutians, no one had to tell me twice. The clouds grew darker and the rain and wind increased in violence. One thing about it was that we didn't have to worry about the Japs, because if they were out there they would have their hands full, just like we were. The storm finally let up, and then I realized that this was the first typhoon I had ever been in. It was scary, and I would just as soon pass on that from now on.

Our job was to give anti-submarine protection, anti-aircraft defense if needed, bombard and help capture small islands at the entrance. The island that was assigned to us was Homonhon. It was a small island and just a few Japs were on it. We did our job, the marines landed, and they took the island in short order.

Our next duty was to defend the minesweeping units as they were clearing the mines for the landing that was to come on the 20th of October.

LEYTE GULF

On the morning of the 18th, the minesweepers started at dawn sweeping the main channel. There were still good-size waves, which made their job more difficult. The plan called for them to sweep all day, then toward evening to head out to the mouth of the channel. On the way out there was an air attack. The Ross laid down a smoke screen, so the enemy could not see the minesweepers and it also help to hide us. The attack didn't last long, so we proceeded on our way. We did get a little off schedule, so when we got to the mouth of the channel, the unit turned around and started back. We were in the main channel where it had already been swept. I was P.O. of the watch on gun 45 from midnight to 0400. We were getting hungry, and the fellows on watch with me figured I would have a better chance of getting something out of the galley to eat than anyone else would. I went to the galley, and they were baking bread. I talked the bakers out of two loaves and some butter. I turned to leave the galley, and there was a terrific explosion that knocked me down. The lights went out. We couldn't see each other, but we talked back and forth to find out if everyone was okay. We got to the hatch of the galley, opened it and we couldn't see a thing. About that time a sailor walked by on the deck. We asked him what had happened, and he didn't know either. I had to get back to my watch station. The Ross had lost its power, all the lights were out. A lot of steam was coming up from below decks, all of the phones were out, and every now and then you could hear someone groan. Almost immediately, the fellows were at their stations getting things patched up. Damage control was bypassing different lines by shutting off some valves, and opening different valves to send the steam where it was needed. They were already rigging phones to the key stations. The medical staff was doing their best, but at this point, they didn't have any electricity, although they did have flashlights. They got the auxiliary generator started, and we had lights in some places and some communications. By this time the word got around that we had hit a mine which had exploded under the forward engine room and the forward fire room, and put both of them out of commission right below the galley. The Captain asked for help from the Division Commander, saying, We have hit a mine and are dead in the water." They were sending a fleet-tug, the USS Chickasaw. While we were waiting for the tug, there we were, sitting in the middle of a minefield, adrift, all alone in the darkness, and with no engines we floated helplessly. It was confirmed that both forward fire room and engine room was flooded. With all their twisted steel, they would no longer be of any use to the ship again. The men that were down there would not be standing any more watches.

    We were struggling to save the ship, jettisoning equipment and shifting stores, even some ammunition. We made preparation to abandon ship, in case it became necessary. Finally the ship ceased to settle. We thought that now we might be able to save her, and also there was a tug on its way to help. After all, it's only been about thirty minutes since the mine exploded, but it seemed like hours.

Again there was another terrific explosion that tore the Ross farther apart. We knew what it was this time. We had hit another mine. We also knew that we had some more shipmates that wouldn't answer roll call again. We just couldn't believe that we could hit two mines with in a half-hour. We hit this one at 0210. The first mine took about 40 feet of the keel, and the second one took another 30 with a short space in between. The ship began listing to port, and the stern went under the water clear up to midships. I went aft to the fantail to get the 20MM guns that were back there and I was standing in water up to my belt. No destroyer (tin cans) ever survived two mine hits. We didn't know whether we would be the first one.

We had no choice but to continue with salvage operations, and again to make preparations to abandon ship. I, for one did not like the idea of abandoning ship. If we did make it to land, we would probably run into some Japs, and be taken prisoners. There was one sailor aboard ship that was at Guadalcanal and the destroyer he was on got sunk. He couldn't swim. He had his life jacket on, and he got into a lifeboat. Later on he was rescued. Well, when the captain gave the order to make preparation to abandon ship, he already had his life jacket on. He helped get the first life raft in the water, and he was the first one in. No one could talk him out of that life raft, until the tug came alongside. Besides, the bow of the ship was still about six feet out of the water. If we didn't hit another mine, or the ship didn't break in two, we still had a good chance of staying afloat. Everybody helped each other. Some men came staggering out of an ammunition handling room all battered and bruised. The doctor did the best he could for them. They lived, but there were three buddies in the same handling room who didn't make it.

    The second explosion was much like the first. This time it exploded, and put out the engine room leaving it a mass of twisted steel and flooding the compartment. The deck above it was hot from escaping steam. Now we had no power except for the auxiliary generator. We were still drifting helplessly in the minefields. Salvage operations continued. Some were helping the hurt and wounded. Some were rigging emergency pumps. Torpedoes and depth charges were going over the side. Of course they were unarmed. Anything that could be moved by hand was thrown overboard. The ammunition was being moved from the port side to the starboard side. We had to move everything from port side to starboard to take as much of the list off as we could. The list stopped at 14 degrees. All of the non-essentials were thrown overboard to lighten the ship. About this time the Captain got on the megaphone and spoke. Now hear this. "The Ross is going to stay afloat. Cease preparations for abandoning ship, and continue salvage work. We are going to take her home." You could feel the change of attitude in the men. I don't believe that they worked any harder, but they were more relaxed, and every now and then someone would come up with a wise remark. All except the guy in the life raft, and he was still there.

We received a message that the tug Chickasaw was about three miles away, and they wanted us to show a light so they could close in. The news sure raised the morale of everyone. There were mixed emotions about turning on a light. We were in enemy waters, just off a Jap stronghold, and the initial landing was a day away. We also wanted to get away from the minefield, and we needed help from anyone who would give it to us. The Captain ordered a signal light turned on. Shortly the Chickasaw (our newfound mammy) came to take us in tow. Their skipper came along our starboard side. They gave us salvage gear, then passed us a towline He hollered over; " We'll have you out of there in no time." Within thirty minutes the Ross was under tow, taking us out of that dangerous minefield He took us up near the Island that we had bombarded the day before. (Homonhon). In the meantime, our paymaster wasn't sure that we were going to stay afloat. So he had taken all the money he had for the payroll, and put it in a mailbag, and threw it aboard Mammy. At this time there was a lot of confusion, and no one paid any attention to the money.

It should be mentioned that the tug Chickasaw (Mammy) came through a minefield to get to us, and then turned around and took us back out. We, the crew of the Ross, will always be grateful to the men of the Chickasaw. Some of the salvage gear they gave us were pumps, that we used to pump out some flooded compartments, and the list began to decrease, and the deck astern was almost out of the water.

We were beginning to feel pretty good about things. The list was taken off, so the ship was riding an even keel, and the main deck was clear of the water. We still had some partly flooded compartments, which included the crews sleeping quarters. If we could get these pumped out; we could ride higher in the water. It looked like we were going to have a good day. Everything was falling into place, the sun was shining, and there was some joking between the fellows.

It didn't last long. I was on the starboard side when I heard an explosion, then the roar of an airplane, coming in on the port side. I went to the port side and saw him drop his second and last bomb. All hands on topside scrambled for cover, but some were in the open when the bomb hit, just short of the port quarter. Fragments sprayed the decks. Two men were seriously wounded, and were treated by the corpsmen, and transferred to another ship where they could get better treatment.

We were at battle stations, mainly anti-aircraft defense, as so much of the ship was flooded or blown up. We were in a position for more Jap planes to hit us. It was decided that this was not a healthy spot. Most of our guns were out of alignment, or completely out of commission. There were no fighting ships near, to help drive off the enemy. We had no air cover, so a move to safer waters was the only thing to do, as we needed company.

We didn't have any power to lift the anchor, so it had to be unshackled and left behind. Mammy took us to a spot near an Island where we dropped our other anchor. We were much closer to the enemy shoreline and also close to the beaches where the action was to take place tomorrow at dawn.

It had been only twenty-four hours since we hit the first mine, and it was about 0900 hours when we had the near-bomb hit. Most of these times the gunners mates were trying to get the guns in alignment with directors. We realized that we could not fire the three after 5" guns as the shock of the recoil from the guns might finish breaking the ship in two. So we concentrated on the two 5" guns that were in the bow of the ship, The 40mm and the 20mm throughout the ship. The 20mm were fired by local control so there was no time spent on alignment. We just had to see that they were ready to fire; some of the 3rd class gunner mates did this. The directors of the 40mm were very close to the guns, so only a few minor adjustments were necessary. I don't mean that this was accomplished in a few minutes, but we did do a good job on them. The two five-inch guns were different. We worked closely with the fire control men. The ship was twisted and it made it difficult to get a good alignment. We got them close enough so that we could live with it.

Before dawn we realized that other ships were coming into the gulf. They were our own invasion forces. As dawn broke we first heard the guns from our friendly ships, and then the explosions on the beach. Salvo after salvo was fired from many destroyers, cruisers, and battleships. The Ross was supposed to have been part of that. Shortly after sunrise Japanese planes were overhead. One plane picked out the tug that stayed behind to pick up our anchor. It was quite a distance astern. Since our after guns were out of commission, there was nothing we could do to help him. We looked on helplessly. We saw an object fall, but no explosion or splash. The pilot pulled out of his dive, them up. He came around on our starboard beam. By this time our forward guns were tracking him. The fire control officer had him in his sights, and opened fire. He came very close and that made one gunners mate very happy, and maybe more. We knew that we had the gun and the director very close in alignment. We also knew that the range finder and the ammunition hoist were together as far as setting the time on the nose fuses.

Almost everyone cheered. The little devil got out of there. The tug that took the bomb hit came along side for help. In her guts was an unexploded bomb that could go off at any time. Our torpedo officer was also a bomb disposal officer. He offered his services, and did the abortion. The Ross' electrician's mates salvaged her flood electrical gear, and she was completely recovered.

The first day there were several air raids, and we fired on those that came close to us. There was a cruiser that got torpedoed. She didn't go down, but had a lot of damage. We had burial services for our shipmates who had lost their lives. I was in charge of the color guard. The chief was supposed to do it but he got me to do it for him. It is a job that nobody really wants.

For a burial at sea in wartime, the shipmate is fingerprinted, put in a canvas bag, with a fifty-four pound projectile, then it is sewed closed. He is laid on a slab covered with the American flag. The captain delivers the service nearest to his faith, as given in the Chaplain's manual. Taps are sounded, the color-guard gives a volley of three shots, as the man goes over the side. That is the way it is supposed to be, but in our case the men had been in the water so long that their bodies were bloated, which made them float. We had to send a boat to retrieve the bodies and put another fifty-four pound projectile in the bag so they would sink. Remember Ferrell, the fellow that we threw overboard at Eniwetok? He was one that was buried that day.

    Remember the money the paymaster put in a mailbag and threw on the deck of mammy? About four days went by, and the paymaster wondered what had happened to the money. He started to inquire about it and asked if anyone knew what had happened to it. They said there was over $100,000.00 in it. Money didn't mean anything out there at this time. No one had seen it or knew anything about it. The paymaster waited about half a day, and Mammy came along side. There the mail bag was right where he had thrown it. For four days men had been walking on it, pulling lines and hoses over the top of it. The bag was getting wet, and no one paid any attention to it.

There were a lot more important things to be concerned with.

Probably the thing we needed most was more electrical power. Our main generator was completely out of commission. Our diesel generator was great, but too small to do the job that was needed. The electricians rigged up switches that could turn the power on and off to the different pieces of equipment. Some of the least important things were not turned on for a day or two at a time. The big thing was that we were unable to have power on the guns and on the galley ranges at the same time. There were days that we were under attack most of the day with no power in the galley. We were eating two meals a day and the meals weren't that bad, at least for the first thirty days. Mammy is the one that kept us going. A tug doesn't have room to carry many supplies, so she is always getting some from larger ships for her own use. For example, she would go to "A" and fill her fresh water tanks, and get all the food that she could, and bring it over to us. Then she would go to ship "B" and do the same thing, but this time she would keep it for herself. The next day she would visit ships "C" and "D". A couple of times she got busy and would miss us for a day or two. Fresh water is what we needed the most.

Remember when I went aboard the Pennsy, and said that fresh water was a precious commodity. Well, we really found out how precious.

My gunnery officer came up with an idea that maybe the army would have a diesel generator that they hadn't put to use yet, and maybe we could get it. The Captain gave his okay to try; so they were getting a working party to go and help bring it back. I told the gunnery officer that I had a brother, who had made the landing when the invasion started, and I would volunteer, but I requested that I have the time to hunt for him. He replied, "Sure, when we get on the beach, but don't get too close to the front lines, and don't get yourself killed or wounded, because we both will be in trouble, and be back here by 1400 hours."

I did get up to about a half-mile from the front lines, and found out my brother Virge had left that morning for the front. That was the last time we were in the same area at the same time. Shortly after I got to the beach, the gunnery officer came with an army truck and a generator. We loaded it into the whaleboat, and headed for the ship. The Captain was very happy.

The generator was hoisted aboard and right away the electricians discovered it had AC current instead of DC, and it was air cooled instead of water-cooled. That didn't stop the electricians and the engineers. They change the wiring and redesigned it to be water cooled, and it worked. It really helped to know that there was power on the guns at all times.

For the next few days it was one air raid after another. Our gunners were getting better all the time, not just our ship, but on all the ships flaming planes became a frequent sight, but a happy one. We were at our battle stations so much that we didn't even secure from General Quarters.

The nights were getting bright, it was almost a full moon and the Japs loved to harass us. The air raids kept coming almost constantly day and night. No one was getting much sleep and it was very wearing. One officer was telling a fellow officer that when he went to sleep, he had trouble finding his helmet when air defense sounded. The other officer suggested that he sleep with his helmet on. He did, and the next morning when he awakened, the left side of his face was paralyzed from sleeping with the helmet on. The edge of the helmet had hit some nerves and paralyzed the left side of his face His nickname became Stone Face.

One evening probably about 1800 hours, part of the crew was in chow line waiting to eat. Air Defense sounded, and a gunners mate 3rd C, came running up to his gun #41 where he was the gun captain. When he was almost there he passed me, and I said, "Calm down, Slim, they're a long ways out there." He asked if I could see them. I answered, "Sure, they are off the port bow bearing 350." Even without looking he said, "If you can see them, they're too damned close." I didn't have the best reputation for identifying planes, and this is what he was referring to.

We felt like we were asking for trouble anchored where we were. There were no friendly ships near enough to help. So it was time to move again.

The Captain got permission to move us amidst other ships, and Mammy moved us again. We got to know the crew real well. We felt safer. You know the old saying, "Misery loves company."

A report came in that many planes were

coming. They were being intercepted by our fighters, but they were headed this way. One of the sights I will never forget is when I counted five Japanese bombers all aflame and all falling at the same time. It was a beautiful sight. There were more than just the five, but they were falling one and two at a time. The only other place one could see this would be in the movies. This was the first time that we had good air coverage. Two of the bombers were trying to get away, and our 5" guns got on them. They trained aft and the muzzle of the gun was almost resting on the bridge. The Exec. was almost looking down the barrel when the gun captain fired. The Exec. and some of the other men went down on the deck. The Exec. crawled off on his hands and knees, not able to see, and he was burned on the face and neck. He was patched up and sent to another ship for further treatment.

There were a couple of small ships that got hit in shallow water and ran aground. They took the men off, and the ships were just setting there. One day a PT boat heard that we were dead in the water, so they came over to see if we had any 50 cal machine guns aboard that we weren't using. I told them we didn't, but if they would come back tomorrow, I would have at least one. I also told them I didn't know what condition it would be in. They said the main thing they needed was a barrel. The next morning I got permission from the gunnery officer to go aboard the ships that had run aground, and get their 50 cal. There were two of us that went, and we brought back six machine guns. That afternoon the PT boat came along side to get the barrel. We had gone over the guns, cleaned and oiled them, putting them in good working order. So we offered to trade with them. They accepted the offer, and the next day they were back. Now they wanted to trade back again. We wanted to know why. They said that they wouldn't have the right serial number on the gun that they were charged with. I had never though of that, so we gave them the one from the other ship, plus their own gun. The word got around the PT boats that we had some 50 cal. machine guns, so we were getting company every day. Finally the word got to me to get rid of whatever I had that the PT boats were coming after. All of the officers aboard knew what they were coming after, but they didn't want to acknowledge it. If they didn't know, they were not in trouble.

Aboard ship there are spare parts for things that might break down, including gun parts. We had three 5" guns that we couldn't fire, so we had some spare parts, and we became a depot. Finally we ran out of spare parts. A gunnery officer from another destroyer needed some parts because he couldn't get two of his guns to operate. We knew how it felt not to be able to have all of our guns operating. This time we received permission to take the parts off from #3 gun mount. We practically stripped the gun, and I forgot to have him sign for them.

The Ross didn't furnish much comfort anymore, with no fresh water for showers, no well-ventilated places to sleep or eat, two meals a day, beans or pancakes for breakfast, lamb for the evening meal. Breakfast would start about 0700 hours and run sometimes until 1100 or 1200, Depending on how many air raids we had. The evening meal started about 1700 hours and ran until everyone was fed, maybe until 2000 hours. The flour had weevils in it, so after it was baked we would pick out the black spots and eat the bread, all the meals were served cafeteria style.

Doc Storrs became concerned about sanitation aboard ship. He ordered that all salt-water bathing be taken forward, and that a head be built aft. It was really something to see. It was constructed out of wood, was a four holer, there were no sides, but it did have a canvas top for shade and some protection from rain and wind. It protruded well over the side. There was no privacy whatsoever. Sometimes it would become a little embarrassing when a native canoe went by, but it was a good place to rest and think. Once in a while a native canoe would pull up to the fantail, and ask to trade Jap souvenirs for food or almost anything. There would always be a lot of fellows who would go back and talk with them. One day a native canoe went to another destroyer, and when they heard a lot of fellows back there talking, they threw some hand grenades aboard ship. They weren't natives, but Japs. It killed some and wounded others. From that day on, no canoes came near a ship. At night we had a whaleboat that circled the ship all night. There were four fellows in the boat and they were armed with 45 pistols and a Thompson sub-machine gun.

Going back to the head: After the head had been constructed for about two weeks, a large ship pulled along the port side, and knocked down the throne. Oh, were we mad!

About this time I thought when has the Thompson sub ever been cleaned? I asked Slim the 3rd c if he had ever cleaned it, and he said he hadn't. Slim and I were the only two that had keys to the small arms locker. So I asked him if he would clean it, and he said he would. In about three minutes he came back and said that there was no Thompson in the whaleboat. We got a list of the men who had the watch for the last week, and tried to find out what had happened to the gun. We finally realized the gun had been missing for at least two weeks, and we never did find out what happened to it. The men on watch were going around the ship protecting it without a gun. I'm sure one of two things happened to it. It either fell over the side of the boat or someone traded it to some native for a souvenir. I had to report it as lost, because I wanted to issue another one for the boat. I merely said it slipped out of my hands when I was going up the ladder, and it fell in the drink.

Everybody was sleeping on topside or in the passageways, even the Captain, some of the fellows even slept standing up. We were sleeping on topside because there was no air below decks. Chief Murphy, three other fellows, and I slept under the overhang on #2 turret. By this time the Exec. was back aboard, and he had decided to make the rounds of the different stations. Well, he caught a lot of officers and enlisted men sleeping, including the chief and I. We were supposed to be at air defense and wide-awake. When he told the Captain, the Captain asked if there was at least one man awake at each station. He was told, "Yes," so the Captain said "forget it."

THE NIGHT OF THE GREAT BATTLE

Rumor had it that the Japs were coming into Leyte Gulf, in three different groups. They had decided to have a showdown. The first group had 39 ships, the 2nd group had 23 ships, and the 3rd group had 14 ships.

Our submarines sighted the 1st group, and sank two heavy cruisers and damaged the third. Now we knew where part of their fleet was. The 2nd group was spotted by carrier planes, and several attacks were made on them.

In preparing for the coming battle, signals were flashed throughout the gulf. PT boats rushed by us on their way to battle. Most of the fighting ships had left the gulf to be in the coming battle. The destroyer squadron that the Ross belonged to was out there except for us. Our Captain did arrange with the skipper of Mammy that in case the enemy should break through, to pull our stern around as we still had four torpedoes, and we could use our forward guns.

My friend, Cecil King GM2/C

was still on the Pennsylvania. My other friend Keith VanCourt, GM1/C from the Robinson was there too. I figured that if my friends do their job well I won't have anything to worry about, but if they don't, I will have more problems than I will be able to handle. They did their job well, otherwise I wouldn't be writing this.

This was probably the greatest torpedo attack by destroyers of all times. Our squadron was in the middle of it. They struck the first and hardest blow at the enemy. One ship from our squadron took hits from our own cruisers as well as the enemy. She received 18 hits in all. She was dead in the water, and another destroyer went along side and lashed the two ships together, and got her out of there. When she finally limped back into Leyte, our

Doctor went over to take care of the wounded, as their doctor had been killed.

One day someone reported three unidentified planes off the port beam. They were identified as twin engine bombers of the Lillies type. Our two 5" guns trained out on them, and as they got within range, they opened up with rapid fire. The Ross had knocked two of them out of the sky before any other ship started to fire. Now we knew darned well our guns were in alignment. That same evening a Zero (fighter plane) came in with machine guns blazing, and got the same fellow in the leg that had reported the three planes that morning. The Doc patched him up and he had to stay off of his leg for a couple of days.

One day we fired nine times at different groups of enemy planes. That day it started shortly after six in the morning and ended around eight that night. So all day long we were at battle stations waiting for the next attack. When they do come, we get all tense. It is almost a relief, as we are not staring into the sky straining our eyes, looking for something that isn't there. And we're glad of it. When they do come, we get very busy. We have seen planes that were hit and in flames falling and out of control, coming down and crashing into one of our ships, and setting it on fire. In case you wonder what burns on a ship made of all steel, the first thing is the paint, and then the flammable liquids, such as diesel fuel and thinners.

The day after the night sea battle, the Japs started using the Kamikazes (suicide planes), along with their bombing runs. We were getting into November, and they started to increase the number of Kamikaze attacks. Every time there was a suicide dive, when it was over, there was one less pilot and one less of the enemy. I would estimate that 60 percent of the suicide pilots missed their targets. Of course, a lot of them died on their way down from the gunfire that was shot at them.

It seemed like whatever ship started firing first at a Kamikaze was the ship that they made their dive on. We only had $2/5^{th}$'s of our big guns working, so we got to the point that we didn't fire at them unless they had a zero target angle on us, meaning that they were coming straight at us.

The Ross was a destroyer, and it was built to carry the war to the enemy. Instead, we sat dead in the water, depending on other ships to protect us, and to provide us with all our needs. It was brought up at different times, that if she had sunk that night, and we were rescued, we wouldn't be sitting out here helplessly. Perhaps we were just feeling sorry for ourselves. It had been weeks of constant air raids and Kamikaze attacks. For some it had been sheer hell, for others it had been fear or outright exhaustion. Regardless of which category the individual fits into, he was under great strain.

Each day we thought we had seen the worst of it. Then we got the word to expect a "typhoon within the next twenty-four hours." No one knew if the Ross could ride out a typhoon. She was sitting low in the water, seventy feet of the keel was missing, two large holes were in her hull, and there was only one anchor to keep us from drifting into another ship. All the hatches were dogged down, and all loose gear was secured.

Before the storm hit, there were mixed

emotions. We didn't like the idea of a typhoon, but it would keep the Japs' aircraft out of the air. The men were huddled in the passageways or any other dry spot they could find. A few of the gunners' mates went with me to the gun shack. It was on the boat deck in the after part of the ship. If the ship was going to break in two, it would be the after part that would sink. We were so tired that we lay down and went to sleep anyway. About two o'clock in the morning, I woke up, and found I was the only one left up there. I lay there for a while listening to the ship moan and creak and groan, and I finally went forward. Once again misery likes company, plus the fact that I was truly frightened.

They told me while I was sleeping that there were two ships that were drifting, and they had almost ran into us, in fact, quite a few small ships had drifted by. They thought the storm was over, because it was so calm. Just about that time, it came over the loud speakers that we were in the eye of the storm, and warned us not to take any unnecessary risks, as we were in for a good blow. In just a few minutes the wind picked up and the rain came down in the buckets full. The wind changed directions so fast, that the ship could not keep her bow into the wind. The ship began to rock from side to side, and the anchor was sliding along the bottom. The ship drifted about a mile before the anchor caught. By the time morning came, we had ridden out our second typhoon.

By late afternoon the air raids were coming in. They had their suicide planes, as well as their bombers. It seemed like every time one looked up, there was an enemy plane up there. They were coming in continually. I was standing with Burchett GM2/C near the smokestack looking at the planes overhead. He said, "Here, have a cigarette" I didn't smoke at this time, but I took one. The ensuing habit lasted for thirty-two years before I realized that I didn't want to smoke anymore.

A merchant ship was requesting that a doctor come over, as they had two very sick men. Our Doc Storrs went over and took care of them. When the Doc came back he told Chief Murphy that they had a 5" gun that wouldn't fire, and asked if someone could help them out. So the Chief asked Fred Hannah, a fire controlman, and me what we could do for them. After talking we found that it had been this way ever since the ship went into commission, and they had been in five different ports that had repair yards, and they had never gotten it repaired. We were able to get it to fire, but if we went more than mid-ship on the port side it would trip the circuit breaker. That part we never did get fixed. When she left Leyte, she went to Luzon, and we heard that she was sunk I always wondered if that gun had been working 100 percent if she might have stayed afloat.

    We began to notice that the number of attacks depended on the weather. If the visibility was poor, we seldom had air raids. We were praying for bad weather especially rain clouds. We would catch the fresh water and use it for shaving, washing the hands and face, and if it looked like a big thundershower, we would take our clothes off and have a shower.

    We had been in Leyte Gulf for a month or so when a supply ship came. The supply officer tried to get some supplies from them, so we could eat a little better. He was told, "Sorry these supplies are for combat ships, and since you are not sea-worthy, you are not classified as a combat ship any longer.

    One day during an attack, our number two 5" gun had mis-fired. This is when the ordnance repair party goes to work. At this time it included Chief Murphy, Burchett GM2/C and me. When we got to the turret we evacuated everyone. At this time we didn't know if we had a misfire or a hang-fire, but we knew that if the barrel is hot from firing, we had to get it out of the gun before it bakes off. This time Murphy opened the breech mechanism. I caught the powder charge, and handed it to Burchett who was on the outside of the turret and he threw it overboard. We had to do the same procedure for the projectile. Everything went like the book said it would. We had just finished the 5", and we were still in the same raid when we got the word that barrel, 1 on gun #44 stopped firing. Burchett and I went on this one. This gun is very hot, but it is an open mount, and the powder and the projectile are in the same case. It is much smaller, about a tenth of the size of the five-inch. I opened the breech and Burchett threw it overboard.

By this time we were in Leyte Gulf longer than any other ship. They had heard about us, and some of them went out of their way to be friendly. A small sub-chaser dropped their anchor near us, and they were going to look after us. A few times during a raid they would lay a smoke screen for us. It did make us feel good, but we couldn't see anything. Whenever there was a raid, they were always shooting their guns, whether the enemy was in range or not. Sometimes they didn't realize how close they were coming to our ships. They ran out of ammunition, and came over to us for some. The Captain said he would give them some, if they promised not to send it back to us in the air.

Our long wait for a floating drydock (Hotkettle 29) was coming to an end. Again, there were mixed emotions. We would be sitting in a floating drydock, and the Japs would love to get two ships for the price of one.

The Gold braid had to consider a possibility of a typhoon. The question, where do we put the drydock? The people on the Ross wanted to stay in the same area as we were, as there was some anti-aircraft protection. The Gold Braid thought we would be better protected from typhoons in a different area. Who do you think won? Our Captain's request for destroyer protection was granted if they became available. They also promised that smoke screens would be laid down on bright, moonlight nights, by small ships. It helped.

When Hotkettle was close enough, we asked if we could get in tomorrow. The reply was, "We are loaded with materials to repair you, and we will try to get you within six days from now." So we had more waiting to do. On the sixth day, we were scheduled to enter the dock at nine o'clock. Two large tugs were on their way to move us in.

Over the radio circuit came the message, "Many enemy planes are headed your way during the next half hour all ships will open fire." One of the merchant ships took a bomb hit. That did a lot of damage and set it on fire.

Our two tugs left us to fight the fire on the merchant ship. The Captain asked for any kind of help to get us in the dock. They sent one very small tug. We missed the entrance the first time, but the second time we got some added help from a Net-Tender and we made it in.

This was the first time Hot Kettle had been in a war zone, and their gunners had very little practice in firing the guns. So a deal was made that we would man their guns. By us manning their guns, their men would be free to work on our ship. By this time we thought we were pretty good shots. Another air raid came in the afternoon, and it was a large one. They struck at our main force. We did not fire at the enemy unless it had a zero target angle and it was within 2,000 yards. Two of their planes survived the attack on our main force, and were headed our way. Our guns were tracking them. They came to 3,000 yards before they changed course. Again we gave a sigh of relief.

That night they pumped the drydock out, and the next morning I went down to see how bad it looked. I wasn't down there long, as it was like a busy beehive with men who knew what they were doing. I did see where the keel was blown away, and the two large holes in the hull. I couldn't imagine how they were going to patch it up to make it sea worthy, or how long it was going to take. They began working on it at once. They had the drydock crew, repairmen from a tender, and a gang from a repair station ashore. They worked day and night. No one wanted to stay on her more than they had to. The small ships laid a smoke screen every night in order to work twenty-four hours a day. They wanted us out of there, and we wanted out.

Some of the fellows said the monsoon season had started. I didn't know about that, but I did know we were getting a lot of rain. We could wash in fresh water, and even wash our clothes in it. It sure cut back on the number of raids that the Japs were making. It just didn't last long enough, because when the skies cleared, the more active the enemy became.

One afternoon Burchett and I were sitting in gun mount #3. I was reading cowboy stories and he was reading comic books.

All of a sudden we heard gunfire. We jumped up and looked out the port hatch. We both thought that this plane was coming right in on us. He was headed right for the hatch that we were standing in. I felt that the only reason he didn't come in was that a shell had exploded near the plane and it changed the course of the plane. I also believe that the pilot was dead even before the shell exploded. The plane went aft of where we were, and it hit the top of our gun mount #5. It was on fire when it hit the inner wall of the drydock. It set the drydock on fire near a 20mm magazine, the ammunition exploded, the engine of the plane went through the drydock, hitting their sick bay, Killing a man, then going into the drink. Two men from the Ross stayed at their 20mm guns until after the plane hit the gun turret, throwing gasoline and flames everywhere, and setting the two men on fire. The flames were quickly put out by wrapping the men in blankets. A LST came along side to help fight the fire. With everyone working the fire was out in twenty minutes. Before the fire was out, we had the second suicide plane coming in just like the first one.

He was actually shot out of the air, and fell into the ocean. Things were getting a little quieter, and we started talking about what had just happened. Someone wondered what had happened to the bomb on the first plane. We all agreed that it had not exploded. Just at that time it was announced that an unexploded bomb was in the basin of the drydock, and to keep clear of it until it was handled. Thank goodness, it was a small one, and two men could handle it. They threw it through a hatch in the drydock. Every day and night, weather permitting, there were either bombing runs or suicide dives.

    Then the day came when the work was all done, the hole in her hull was patched, and she would float again. We were anxious to get underway and out of Leyte Gulf, it didn't happen that way. They filled the dock, we were afloat and Mammy hauled us out, it was a relief to get out of the dock. The enemy planes kept coming all the time we were waiting for a departure date. One convoy sailed, but we had to wait for a slower one. Our tow was a merchant vessel, and it was not used to towing another ship. We had to be in a slow moving convoy so they could keep up.

On the morning of December 19, 1944 we hoisted anchor and got under way. A tug was our power until she could get us hooked up to the ship that was going to tow us. There was a warning that another typhoon was on its way; we had trouble making the hookup, as the waves were a little rough. We finally made it, and now we were on our way home. Things were beginning to go our way; the typhoon was swinging to the north. There was a taskforce to the north of us and they got the full blast of the typhoon. They lost three destroyers that capsized. Over seven hundred men want down with their ships. They were the Hull, the Spence, and the Monagham.

It was the 19th of December, just two months or sixty-one days ago that we hit the mines. Now we were going almost over the same spot, It gave me a weird feeling. We were at sea for Christmas, heading for Hollindia, the first stop on our way home. On Christmas Eve, the captain and the doctor came up with the idea of using some of the medicinal whiskey and they made some punch, it was very good and everyone enjoyed it. I don't think it was the punch nearly as much as it was the thought behind it. When I left Pearl Harbor in December of 1941, I was at sea for Christmas, too. On New Years Eve this year we entered Hollandia.

One of the first duties anyone had after dropping anchor, was for the supply officer to hunt for some decent food, he sure did his job. On New Years Day, we had turkey and all the trimmings, including pie.

The next day we were underway to go to Manus, when we got there they gave us a warm welcome. We stayed there for a few days, then we were on our way to Pearl, this was going to be a long trip, there wasn't much to do except to stand watches. The duty section was four hours on and eight hours off.

One day Burchett and I were back in #3 gun mount reading cowboy stories and comic books, ---maybe the same ones as before, or maybe some other ones. The assistance division officer came over and said, "DuBois, where is Smith working?" I told him which gun he was on, he left for about a minute and came back and said, "DuBois, where is Jones working?" So I told him which gun he was on, he had been gone only about a minute and he came back the third time and said, "DuBois where is Brown?" Now you must realize that every time he interrupted me, I lost my place in the book I was reading, I slammed the book together and said, "What the hell is this, a game?" That made him angry, and he said, "When I ask you a question, you answer it." I thought for a moment, and said, "Sir, your answer is, I don't know." He said, "You know where he is, now where is he?" "Sir, I don't know." The funny part of the whole thing is that he turned to Burchett and said, "Where is Brown working?" Burchett turned up the palm of his hands, shrugged his shoulders, and said," If DuBois doesn't know, I don't know." He was furious with us and it was a couple of days before he would talk with us.

    All departments had to make out a list of the equipment that they were charge with, but did not have now, and tell what had happened to it. Our #3 handling room was hit pretty badly, so whatever we were short, we had it in there. All of the spare parts that we gave away and even the parts that we took off the guns or ships were in there. Anyone that knew anything about guns or ships would know it was impossible to have that much equipment in one handling room. I turned in the report, and never heard a thing about it. Even in wartime they had to have their damned paper work.

    The trip back to Pearl was uneventful. We had two concerns. Our tow cable parting, and our fresh water supply. We had five broken cables from Leyte to Pearl, about one every thousand miles. The water held out well. We ran into quite a few rain squalls, which helped on the water supply. We traveled between four and eight knots, depending on the weather, wind, and how rough it was. We were only in Pearl a couple of days, just long enough to take on supplies, mainly chow, fresh water, and some of our mail caught up with us.

In my mail there was a letter from my oldest brother, Duke.

He was stationed in Luzon in the Philippines. After taking on our supplies we headed for San Francisco, the greatest liberty town on the West Coast.

When coming into San Francisco, The water is generally rough when approaching the entrance. It was rough the day we came in, and we broke our tow cable. It took us a couple of hours to hook up again.

It was March 1st when we went under the Golden Gate Bridge. The bridge was always something to see, but it sure meant more this time. We headed right for Mare Island Navy Repair Yard.

SUMMARY

One year and seven days ago the USS ROSS was commissioned. A green crew was trained, participated in the landings on Saipan, Tinian, Palau, Ulithi, Leyte Gulf, and the Philippines. In sixty-one violent action-packed days, we endured 286 air raids, and numerous Kamikaze attacks, received eleven hits and one Kamikaze. We were hit by two typhoons, hit two mines, (to this point the only destroyer to hit two mines and stay afloat), and also to this point made the longest tow job in Navy history. We were 71 days from Leyte Gulf to San Francisco, Which was over 7,500 miles at 4 to 6 knots

Shortly after the ship was secured to the dock, we moved into barracks. We were living like civilians. We would get up in the morning, eat breakfast, and be on the ship by eight o'clock, then back to the barracks by five. We only got the duty every four days. Sometimes we wouldn't get a watch, so we would have the evening to ourselves, but could not leave the area.

A week after we got there, they started to give leave to the men. I got a thirty-day leave and went home. It sure was nice to be home with Mother's cooking. She certainly cooked better than they did in the Navy.

After coming back from leave, my watch station was to check the men in as they came aboard in the morning. This one morning two fellows didn't report in. One was a gunners mate; the other one was a deck hand. When the time came to report to the office, I reported all men present or accounted for. Two hours later the shore patrol was bringing the two men aboard. I was called to the office, and they asked me about this. I said that it is a mad house in the morning down there and I thought they had hollered out their names, so I checked them as being present. They knew it was a story, and told me not to let it happen again.

One night I had the duty, but no watch. I couldn't see any sense of staying in the area, so I told a gunners mate that I was going on the beach. If he needed me I would be at Chief Murphy's. About ten o'clock he came after me. They had changed the watch schedule. I had a twelve to four watch and I had better get back. In the service it isn't so much what you do, It's what you get caught doing.

In April Captain Coe was transferred to Boston. Commander Raney relieved him as captain of the Ross. We had quite a few officers and other men transferred from the ship. It took the yard workmen 806,000 man-hours over a period of 110 days to get the Ross ready for sea duty and possibly more action. She was as good as new with the exception of a vibration at high speeds.

In June of 1945, the Ross started all over again with a shake down cruise and a lot of new crew members. By July 15th we were back in Hawaii. Some of our better 1st/c and chief petty officers were transferred. Chief Murphy and Burchett 1st/c gunners mate was transferred. I hated to see those two go, as all three of us had become very good friends. When we had a problem the three of us could come up with a solution. By Murphy being transferred, that made me the senior gunners mate aboard, so I had charge of the gang.

When we left Hawaii we headed west to

some old familiar places. Most of them I would have just as soon forget, but we were headed for enemy waters, for more action. We missed the fighting of Iwo Jima and Okinawa, Thank God. We were off from Okinawa when a lookout spotted what he thought was a mine, and sure enough it was a mine that had broken away from its anchor. It would float until something would explode it. It was too dangerous just to let it float. The Captain said to explode it. It was an object about three feet in diameter with a lot of little sensors sticking out all over it. Only about 1/3 of it was out of the water, and it was bobbing in the water. At the same time our ship is rocking and rolling, and we are a long ways from it. At first we used 30 cal. rifles, trying to hit those little sensors with no luck. Then we used the 20mm guns, and finally with the 40mm guns, someone got lucky.

About this time my gunnery officer asked me to take a test for chief gunners mate. I told him I had already qualified once, and I wasn't going to do it again. He said, "You know if you don't make chief that they will probably transfer another chief over to us." He asked me to go down and sign my name to the examination sheet. Which I did and that is the way I made chief.

A few days after the mine incident, we were cruising west going toward Japan. The Ross was assigned Picket Duty. Being assigned Picket Duty was almost the kiss of death. Then we received a report that an atomic bomb had been dropped on two cities in Japan. It was ten to twenty times more powerful than anything we ever had. We had never heard of an atomic bomb, so we could not visualize what they were saying. A few days after that some of our airplanes flew overhead, and I believe they did every trick in the book. I thought to myself, Boy, these guys are in trouble, because someone will report them. About this time it came over the speaker system that the Japs had surrendered. The planes probably put on the greatest air show ever, at least to us. Two days later we sailed into Yokohama Bay.

We were one of the first ships to make liberty there, I felt a little uncomfortable because of the "chief" uniform, and I hadn't gotten used to it yet. Every time we met a Jap service man he would salute, and of course, we saluted back. I went on the beach with Tim, the one I had crossed the equator with, in fact I had on one of his uniforms. Whenever we met a Jap service man, he would get off the sidewalk and go to the middle of the street. He didn't even accidentally want to bump into us. The civilians were polite, but very standoffish, as they were afraid of us. Whatever store we went into, there was someone in there that we could communicate with enough to buy what we wanted, knowing how much it cost. Of course, there were some Americans that made an ass of themselves, mostly by making the civilians walk in the street. The other thing I never forgot was how low their latrines were built to the floor, this was in their Naval Academy. Our liberty was for only three hours, from one to four, and we had better be aboard by then. The big wheels didn't want trouble of any kind. There were only a few that could go on liberty at a time, we had to go in pairs. Nobody trusted anybody, but we wanted to see how they lived,

We rode out another typhoon while we were in Yokohama Bay. We had been warned that there was one on the way, this time we were prepared, the captain had steam up and both anchors out. When the storm hit they put power on the screws, and the screws were turning at seven knots, and we were staying in the same place, some of the other ships were not as prepared, and they were drifting, one destroyer drifted down on us. I was standing a watch that night, and I could see it was going to hit our ship where I used to sleep before I made chief. I went to the hatch and hollered, "Get out of there, a ship is drifting down on us and it's going to hit in this compartment." I had other duties, so I turned to leave, about seven minutes later I went back to the hatch, and I was saying, "You guys had better get the hell out, -- never mind, it's too late now." CRASH! I guess you know I didn't have to tell them again to get out, it was like a stampede going by. The anchor of the other ship put a hole in the compartment where these guys were; it was probably six to eight inches above the water line. We had fenders out trying to keep the two ships from hitting each other, because they would have beaten themselves to death. Even then as she slid down our port side, we lost both the boat davit and the captain's gig. She finally drifted past our fantail. We left Japan the early part of September 1945, our first port of call was Hawaii, our second port was Bremerton. It must have been an uneventful trip, as I don't remember it.

We arrived in Bremerton the first part of December. The Executive officer had been transferred from the ship when we were in Hawaii to take command of his own ship. We met in Bremerton and he wanted me to request a transfer to his ship, I thanked him, but no way would I want that duty, he was the same officer who kicked me off the bridge, of course he had every right to do it. I was out of line.

My Dad had four cousins who lived in Seattle, they were probably in their seventy or eighties, two of them never married, they were very good to me. I ate at their house a few times, they offered me a room, but I never accepted. I did have Christmas dinner with them, and it was nice to be with a family again.

A friend aboard ship, Wayne Edmonds 2/c ship fitter, was fixing me up with a date on January 25, 1946. Her name was Shirley Jorgenson, that night I asked her to marry me, she thought I was crazy, like I told her, when I see what I want, I go after it, she was what I wanted.

We were engaged February 10th, I left on February 15th for San Diego. She arrived in San Diego on April 1st, and we were married on the 6th of April, 1946.

I never thought of this until now, but she came to San Diego on April Fools Day. I wonder if she was trying to tell me something.

Our trip to San Diego was a routine trip, except we were going to put the USS Ross out of commission, for two years she had been my home. We went many places together and had seen many things, we had good times, and we had some bad times, but she always took care of me, and she brought me home. While she was doing this for me, I met fellows who became my friends, they knew more about me than my own brothers, they knew me when things were going well, and they knew me when things were rough, they knew some of my fears, and some of my expectations. They even had an idea of what I wanted out of life. Aboard a smaller ship, one gets close to their shipmates because each one knows the other well, and they are together for a long period of time. There were only a few of the original crew members left aboard, some had been killed, some wounded, and the majority had been transferred to other ships or stations.

Getting the ship ready for the mothball fleet, as it was known, took us about three months, we had certain things that had to be done. I had a book from the Bureau of Ships from Washington, DC telling exactly what to do for the guns. After two months, a Rear Admiral and his staff from the San Diego Navy yards came over to inspect the work that we were doing, the staff gunnery officer found all kind of things that I was doing wrong, by the San Diego Navy yards book. My gunnery officer got the Admiral, and they, together with the staff gunnery officer, and I went down to the chief quarters to find out what went wrong. The three of them were discussing it, when they said I had done something wrong, my gunnery officer would ask me why I had done it like I had and not gone by the book, I told him I had gone by the book. This came up five or six times, finally someone wanted to know what book I was going by. I told him that it was the book sent out of the Bureau of Ships from Washington, DC, my gunnery officer wanted to know if I still had the book, I told him it was in my locker, he asked me to get it. When I brought it back and handed it to him, he looked at the date and checked who had signed it, the date was thirty days before the one from San Diego, and it was signed by a Vice Admiral. Up until now the San Diego crew wanted us to undo everything we had done, and do it their way. When my gunnery officer saw who had signed it, he said, "With all due respect, Sir, I am going along with the Vice Admiral, and my chief gunners mate." I don't think the Admiral was put out as much as the staff gunners officer.

It is the custom in the Navy that anyone, who was aboard ship when it was commissioned, and had stayed on it until it was decommissioned, received the last flag that it flew. I think there were twenty-two of us that qualified so we drew for it, and I received the flag. The Union Jack was cut up and everyone received two stars from it.

I was transferred from the Ross that day, and went aboard the U.S.S. Stanley, it was tied up to the same dock about four ships down from the Ross, the two ships were of the same class of destroyers so they were almost alike. The crew had already been transferred, but there was about a month's work to be done on her, there was no watch section. We came aboard at eight in the morning, went to the mess hall for noon chow, back to the ship after chow, and worked until four, then I went home, Shirley and I having rented a room at a motel to live in.

I got acquainted with the chief gunners mate that was on the ship next to me, we would have coffee together and compare notes about our work. One day he didn't show up for work and no one knew anything about him. Two weeks later he came back aboard, so I hollered over at him and asked, "How's things going?" So he came over to where I was and said, "How in the hell do you think they would be going with two hundred fifty-one inches of cold steel shoved in the cheeks of my ass?" He had been in the hospital with a venereal disease, and he multiplied the length of the needle by the number of shots he took, and came up with two hundred fifty-one inches. Another week later I was transferred to another destroyer that had about two weeks of work left on it. From there I went to the receiving station for separation from the Navy.

I had 120 days of leave coming to me, but they would only pay for 60 days in cash, but would let me go on leave for 60 days, after that they would mail my discharge to me. So altogether I had 6 years, 2 months, and 2 days in the service.

Honorable Discharge front

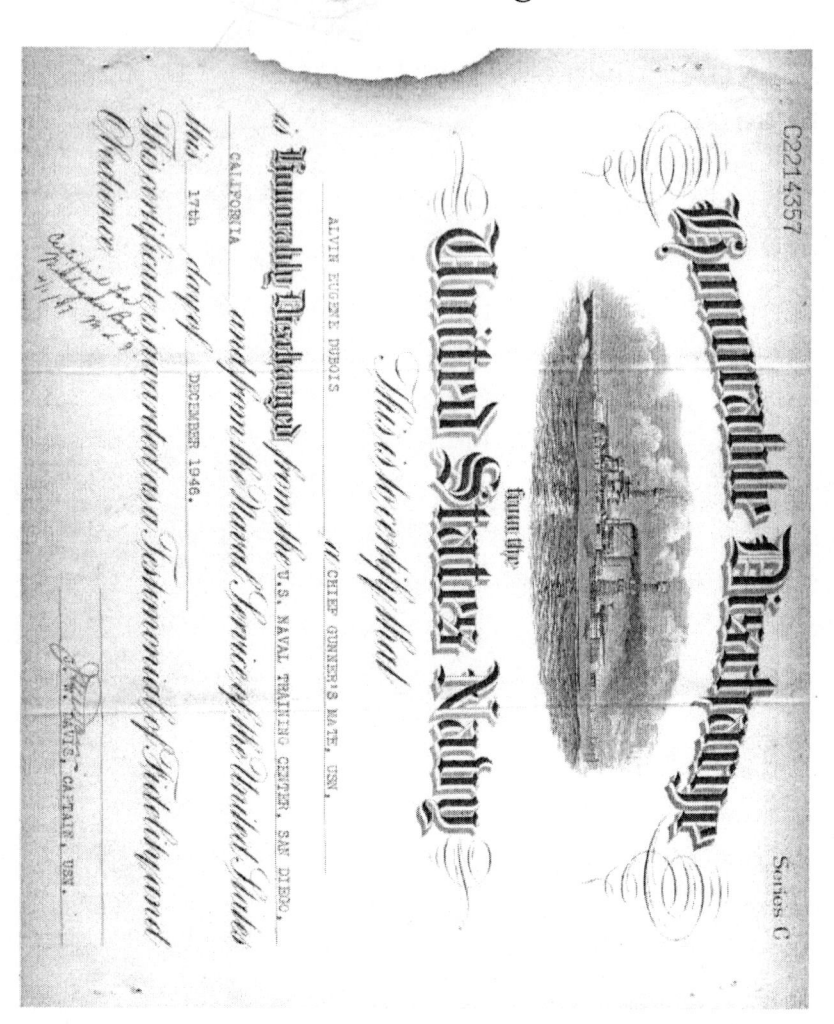

Honorable Discharge

from the

United States Navy

This is to certify that

ALVIN EUGENE DUBOIS

is Honorably Discharged from the U.S. NAVAL TRAINING CENTER, SAN DIEGO, CALIFORNIA *and from the Naval Service of the United States*

this 17th *day of* DECEMBER 1946.

This certificate is awarded as a Testimonial of Fidelity and Obedience

A CHIEF GUNNER'S MATE, USN.

F. KATZ, CAPTAIN, USN.

C2214357

Series C

Honorable Discharge back

NOTICE OF SEPARATION FROM THE U. S. NAVAL SERVICE

311 52 34
DU BOIS, Alvin Eugene
Chief Gunners Mate   USN

1806 13 Mile Road
Royal Oak, Michigan

Place of Separation: U. S. Naval Training Center, San Diego 33, California

Character of Separation: Honorable

1806 13 Mile Road
Royal Oak, Michigan

Race: W   Sex: M   Marital Status: Married   U.S. Citizen: Yes

Date and Place of Birth: 7/13/21 Royal Oak, Michigan

Home Address: 1808 13 Mile Rd. Royal Oak, Mich.

Means of Entry: Enlisted

Date of Entry Into Active Service: 10/16/40

Date: 10/16/40

Place of Entry Into Active Service: NRS, Detroit, Michigan

Ratings Held: AS S2 S1 GM3 GM2 GM1 CGMA CGM   10/1/46

Foreign Service WWII: Yes

Qualifications: None

Service Schools Completed: USNTS, Advance Gunnery Sch. Washington, D. C.   Weeks: 8

Service Vessels and Stations Served On:
N.S. Great Lakes, Ill.
USS PENNSYLVANIA
USS ROSS
USS STANLEY

Remarks:
Asiatic-Pacific (6) Stars
American Area
Philippine Liberation (2) Stars
American Defense (1) Star
World War II Victory Medal
Good Conduct

Signature 1st Direction of Commanding Officer:
F. A. BUNTIN, LT., (jg) USN

Name and Address of Last Employer: Self
From: Self
Main Civilian Occupation: Electric Hydraulic

Job Preference: Construction work, Detroit, Michigan
Preference for Additional Training: On the Job Training
Vocational or Trade Courses: Machines

Off Duty Educational Courses Completed: None

Date of Separation: 12/17/46
Signature of Person Being Separated: Alvin Eugene Du Bois

Letter from James Forrestal

THE SECRETARY OF THE NAVY
WASHINGTON

January 10, 1947

My dear Mr. Du Bois:

    I have addressed this letter to reach you after all the formalities of your separation from active service are completed. I have done so because, without formality but as clearly as I know how to say it, I want the Navy's pride in you, which it is my privilege to express, to reach into your civil life and to remain with you always.

    You have served in the greatest Navy in the world.

    It crushed two enemy fleets at once, receiving their surrenders only four months apart.

    It brought our land-based airpower within bombing range of the enemy, and set our ground armies on the beachheads of final victory.

    It performed the multitude of tasks necessary to support these military operations.

    No other Navy at any time has done so much. For your part in these achievements you deserve to be proud as long as you live. The Nation which you served at a time of crisis will remember you with gratitude.

    The best wishes of the Navy go with you into your future life. Good luck!

Sincerely yours,

James Forrestal

James Forrestal

Mr. Alvin Eugene Du Bois
1808 13 Mile Rd.
Royal Oak, Michigan

Letter from President Truman

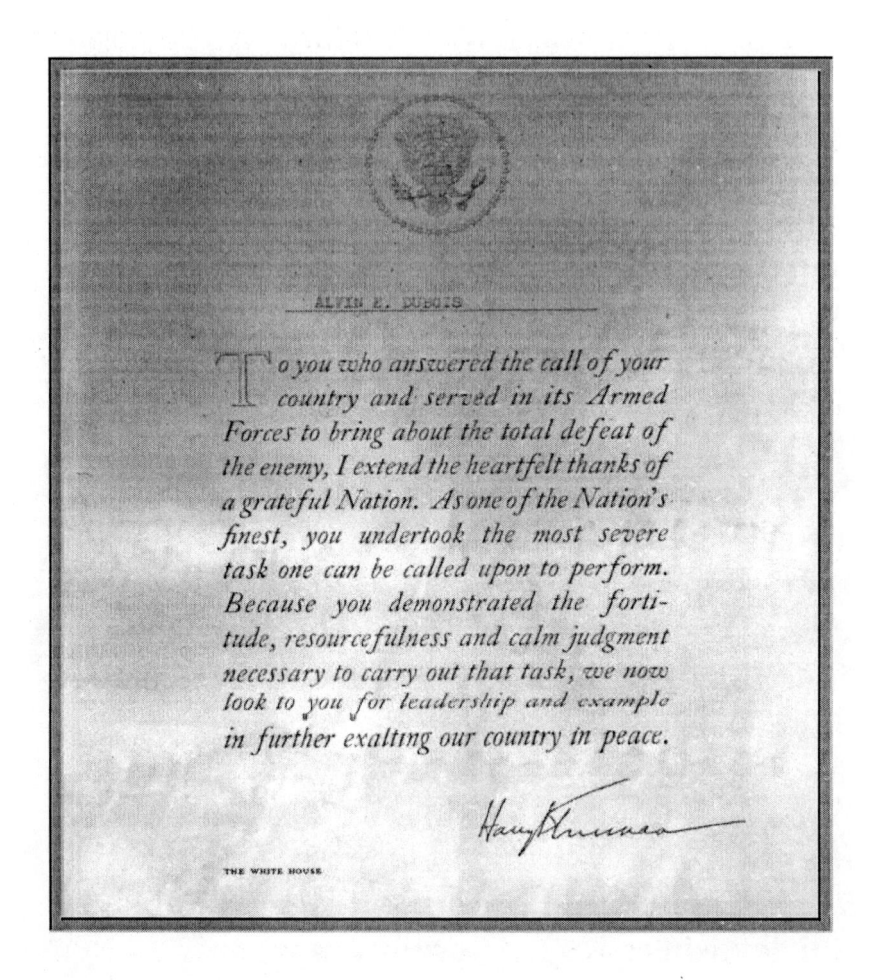

ALVIN E. DUBOIS

To you who answered the call of your country and served in its Armed Forces to bring about the total defeat of the enemy, I extend the heartfelt thanks of a grateful Nation. As one of the Nation's finest, you undertook the most severe task one can be called upon to perform. Because you demonstrated the fortitude, resourcefulness and calm judgment necessary to carry out that task, we now look to you for leadership and example in further exalting our country in peace.

Harry Truman

THE WHITE HOUSE

CONCLUSION

I joined the Navy with a fellow by the name of Roger Bergin. We had known each other for about three years. I knew he was from Saskatchewan, Canada, and he moved to a small town near Flint, Michigan when he was fourteen, and was raised by an Uncle. When he was about nineteen he moved to Royal Oak Michigan and that is where I met him. That is all I knew about his background.

When he was 22 and I was 18 we joined the Navy. I screwed up on my application and left a week later then he did. Well he drew the Battleship USS Arizona and I got the USS Pennsylvania. He was killed on December 7, 1941 that is the end of the story until December 8, 1991.

My wife, my sister and myself were on the Arizona Memorial looking for his name on the list of the men who died on her on December 7th, 1941. I couldn't see it and kept asking Shirley where Roger Bergin's name was. A lady standing beside of me said that she had a brother-in-law by the name of Roger Bergin who was killed on December 7, 1941. At first I couldn't believe it, until I asked her where she was from, and she was from Canada, then what part of Canada, she replied Saskatchewan. At that point I knew there had to be a connection. I told her my name and I was the guy that Roger joined the Navy with. She recognized my name and got excited. Her husband was sick and stayed at the hotel that day, but she was with another brother-in-law, and she wanted me to stay right where I was until she could get him. She was back within a minute with Roger's brother. The first thing he said was, "Al DuBois, I have looked for you for 50 years." Roger had told them about me in a letter.

FATE-- There were thousands of people that visited the Memorial on December 7th and 8th, and only 150 can get in the motor launch at one time, and we met there for the first time. They don't even have a picture of him. I have two pictures of him and will send them copies. This was worth the trip to Hawaii. I have since sent them the copies of the pictures and have heard from them.

INDEX

27th of December 1940 26
6th of April, 1946 213
Admiral Kimmel 39
Aleutian Islands 101, 103, 110
Apprentice seaman 19, 24
April 1st 213
ASSUMPTIONS 14
Attu 101
Black Cat Cafe 41, 42, 46
Boxing 47, 49, 50
Bremerton 20, 26, 92, 113
Burchett 190, 191, 195, 199, 200
Cassin 66, 69, 72, 78
Catapult 33, 34, 35
Cecil King 96, 97, 183
Censored mail 89
Christmas 26, 56, 84, 198, 211
December 7 .... 82, 84, 135, 224
December 7th 1941 .... 61, 224
December 8, 1991 224
Declassified document 72
Deep-Sea Diving 91
Downes 66, 69, 72, 78
Duke 202

Facts about the USS PENNSYLVANIA BB38
FLEET FLAGSHIP 29
February of 1943 98
Ferrell 142, 170
Fisher 63, 64, 90
Ford Island 27, 61, 66, 68, 73
GM Cook 97
Great Lakes 6, 9, 20, 118
Hawaii 26, 27, 31, 51, 61
Hennesey 57
Holly Stone 25
Honorable Discharge back 221
Honorable Discharge front 220
Joe Bennett 47, 48, 114
Join the Navy 4
July 4, 1941 .... 53, 54
Letter from James Forrestal 222
Letter from President Truman 223
Liberty ....
14, 28, 39, 46, 48, 50, 61, 84, 96, 104, 114, 115, 142
Long Beach 51, 91, 98
Memorial 224, 225
Menu 42, 53, 55
Midway 87

Murphy	141
Pappy Lyons	96
Pat Othout	4, 5, 122
Pay and Expenses	9
Pearl Harbor	71, 84, 88, 135, 199

Pennsy...20, 21, 24, 28, 29, 39, 51, 63, 64, 66, 69, 72, 73, 74, 75, 76, 78, 183

Recruiter	4, 5
Refuel at sea	33

Roger Bergin...4, 5, 6, 20, 28, 29, 39, 46, 61, 70, 71, 88, 224, 225

Royal Hawaiian Hotel	40
Royal Oak, Michigan	6, 117
Seaman 1st class	50
September 1942	90
Shaw	66, 67, 72
Shirley Jorgenson	212, 213, 224
Striking the bells	27
Tennessee	66
Thanksgiving	55, 56
Tokyo bombed	87
Tom Gibson	49
Treasure Island	123, 124, 126, 128
USS Arizona	20, 28, 39, 65, 66, 71, 135, 224

USS Ross...120, 124, 127, 129, 133, 137, 149,

161, 168, 169, 178, 182, 184, 186, 196, 206, 208, 215, 217
Utah 68, 135
VanCourt...57, 102, 104, 105, 108, 112, 115, 116, 119, 183
Virge 172, 173
War games 38
West Virginia 66
Whaleboat 68
Winsette 57, 86
Woodward 98, 99

Copyright © 1996
All rights reserved
No part of this book may be used or
reproduced in any manner what-so-ever
without written permission, except in the case
of brief quotation.
For information, address:

Alvin E. DuBois   *Mrs Shirley DuBois*
6535 N.E. 1st Lane
Ocala, Florida 34470

231

IN LOVING MEMORY OF
Alvin Eugene DuBois

DATE OF BIRTH
July 13, 1921
Clauson, Michigan

DATE OF DEATH
March 29, 2003
Ocala, Florida

SERVICES
Thursday, April 3, 2003
at 10:00 AM
Ft. King Presbyterian Church

OFFICIATING
Rev. James Bullock, Jr.

Please visit "The Family Guestbook"
@www.robertsfuneralhomes.com